PETAIN: VERDUN TO VICHY

Adolf Hitler and Petain exchanging greetings, just before their first conference in France. Winter, 1940. (*Photo by Dever, from Black Star*)

PETAIN

Verdun to Vichy

BY FRANCIS MARTEL

E. P. DUTTON & COMPANY, INC.

NEW YORK, 1943

43688

DEDICATION

To YOU, my 500,000 comrades-in-arms of the horizon-blue army whose blood, shed at Verdun, cemented the pedestal of Henri-Philippe Pétain.

ACKNOWLEDGMENT

THE AUTHOR is grateful to the following publishers for permission to quote briefly from their copyrighted works:

Reynal & Hitchcock, Inc., for *The Making of Tomorrow*, Raoul de Roussy de Sales, and *Is Tomorrow Hitler's?* H. R. Knickerbocker.

L. B. Fischer, for *Prisoners of Hope*, Howard Brooks.

Editions de la Maison Français, for *Français, Voici La Vérité*, Henri de Kérillis.

Harcourt, Brace & Co., Inc., for Georges Clemenceau, *The Grandeur and Misery of Victory*, Trans. by F. M. Atkinson.

CONTENTS

FOREWORD

THE STORY of Marshal Pétain is the story of human weaknesses, nursed in the loneliness of an essentially self-contained nature, watered and fed by the bright mirage of power and the calculated flattery of schemers. It is a bitter story for Frenchmen to contemplate but it is well for us to remember that the Marshal is not the first, nor is he likely to be the last, great man to fall from great heights into the depth of treachery. Benedict Arnold too was a great man, heaped with honors. And before Judas could become a synonym for betrayal he was one of the Twelve chosen by Christ. The crowded history of France herself contains many great and tarnished names of heroes turned traitor. And France has survived them all, just as she will survive the last and most ancient of her unfaithful sons.

It is superficial to assume that all traitors are petty rogues, marked plainly by the itching palm and the shifty eye. Betrayal is not always a simple choice between good and evil, a conscious and cynical seeking of the easy path to profit and power. The elements of treachery are present in every man's soul, and in no other area of dishonor is the means of self-deception so readily available, the hypocrite's mask so smooth and well-fitting.

The story of Marshal Pétain is one that carries with it the salutary shock of cold truth. And the truth brings always its own bleak comfort. In this case it is the realization that even

9

a France defeated and forsaken is no land of spiritual decay, no home of cowards and dreamers, sheltering behind the senile mask of a plotting old man. It is a nation awake and aware of its betrayal by an erstwhile hero who has proved to the world that prestige can be built upon a myth and that no accumulation of years and honors can appease the insatiably scheming heart.

PETAIN: VERDUN TO VICHY

BOOK ONE

●

THE WHY

CHAPTER 1

THE ROAD TO VERDUN

I HAVE KNOWN Henri Philippe Pétain for most of my life. Our acquaintance was never intimate, or even particularly friendly. In the first place a gap of forty years separated us. Furthermore our paths, social, political and professional, were decidedly divergent. Nevertheless we met frequently in a casual fashion throughout many years until I left France in 1940. And there remains in my mind a curiously complete picture of this soldier, youthfully middle-aged when I met him, cautiously gallant toward my mother and my pretty sisters, polite to my then influential uncles and their still more influential friends.

This picture has aged, without materially changing, in the twenty-five years since Verdun, where I met the Marshal again under circumstances dramatically different from those of my childhood. And this encounter, at the scene of France's dearly bought triumph, was the last occasion upon which the rapidly mounting general showed me a friendly personal recognition. My family idolized Clemenceau; Pétain despised him. And following the Clemenceau Cabinet of 1907, which resulted in General Foch's appointment as dean of L'Ecole Supérieure de Guerre and the subsequent discomfort of Pétain, his visits to our more liberal political circle decreased. During the later years of the war, when Foch was promoted

over the head of Pétain and the latter had several times to
endure the sharp lash of the old Tiger's tongue, they ceased
altogether. And although my mother had known Mme. la
Maréchale, both as Mlle. Hardon and later as Mme. Deherain,
the acquaintance never again progressed beyond the stage of
bows in public.

But the number of occasions on which I could watch and
marvel over the developing career of the Marshal have been
many. The first one, somewhere around my fifth birthday,
was at the home of a favorite uncle. Major Pétain, then in his
late forties, was extremely handsome, polite and rather silent,
except when complimenting the ladies in a somewhat florid
and elderly style. My main reason for noticing him at all was
that the favorite sport of my cousins and myself, that of
inspecting the rows of campaign ribbons across the tunics of
the well-decorated heroes of colonial campaigns and of demanding the appropriate stories to match each one, was impossible to indulge with Major Pétain, who simply had no
ribbons. It had not seemed to us even possible that a soldier
could arrive at the rank of major without a chestful of ribbons,
and so we demanded explanations as soon as politeness would
permit.

"Major Pétain," my father told us, "is not a fighting officer
like our other friends. He is a theoretician, a teacher of the
art and science of war, and these do not win medals."

We debated this, I remember, with some interest. For it
was fascinating to know that war had its art and science; that
it could be taught in a classroom like any other plague of the
small boy's life and was not learned, in full cry, among the
plunging excitements of the battlefield.

A few similar but less heeded meetings preceded the one

at Verdun, which happened during a surprise inspection at the airport where I was stationed. It was brief and meaningless, despite the envy of my comrades and their belief that dizzying promotions would probably pave my pathway through war with ribbons and stars. But it was at least amiable: "Ah, and so this fine young aviator is my old friend Francis! And how are your kind parents?" "They are well, thank you, *mon général.*" And that was all.

Later there were others. There was Pétain as the idol of the French people, receiving smiles from great ladies and flowers from little girls. There was Pétain at the time of his marriage, which might have seemed mildly scandalous in a less exalted figure, since after a lifetime of prudent bachelorhood the newly made Marshal married a middle-aged lady who had quietly obtained an annulment—divorce would still have been frowned upon in the semiclerical circles in which both moved —of her earlier marriage to a moderately well-known sculptor.

At seventy the Marshal seemed curiously, inscrutably ageless. His health was excellent, his figure and features as well known and loved by Frenchmen as those of Napoleon himself. He could grow quickly angry at a seeming discourtesy or contradiction, but the only change of expression was a quick flash of the ice-blue eyes, a tightening of the thin lips beneath the carefully tended mustache. This expression came often during the days of the Daladier cabinets where frequently I would meet him in the anteroom of the Premier's offices, mouth compressed, hands occasionally trembling slightly, but with a firm step, a direct gaze and now no flicker of friendliness; merely a perfunctory greeting or an acknowledging bow. The Marshal did not waste much time upon people who were neither admirers nor subordinates.

This book does not pretend to be an orthodox biography of Marshal Pétain. Its aim is rather to seek out and to show the influences within and without his life which have caused him, at an age when most men are ready and willing enough to meet death, to betray his country to her enemies for the sake of vindicating old hatreds and of appeasing old jealousies. This is not a matter that can be measured in terms of dates and places, except insofar as the dates and places have contributed their share toward corrupting the soul.

A curious sidelight upon the thinking of Pétain is that out of a lifetime of eighty-eight years almost no formal documentation emerges. The customary collection of names, places, dates, details and anecdotal trivia which ordinarily accumulate during half a century around the career of even a moderately great man are curiously absent in the case of Pétain. Behind the imposing façade of the past thirty years, which has produced its own collection of incidents and dates, one finds merely a blank wall on which are inscribed, with statistical brevity, simply the dates and the places which must become matters of public record. It is only by a patient sifting through the dust of that earlier half century, by extracting a name here, a time there, by relating them to a memory or a date, and by placing the whole together upon the sturdier fabric of history that anything approaching a dimensional portrait of this bitter and complex being can be made to emerge from its self-imposed secrecy.

The Marshal, quite simply, hated all references to his early and humble beginnings. Official histories, those which, as an Academician and a public character, he could control through more or less discreet hints, such self-edited accounts as those in Who's Who or in general encyclopedias, begin almost invariably with the bare statement that Henri Joseph Omer

Benoni Philippe Pétain was born on May 23, 1856, at Cauchy-la-Tour; that after a religious-school education he entered the military academy of Saint-Cyr at the age of twenty. Thus in about two lines are compressed the twenty most fateful years of a man's life. There is no mention of his parents, of the occupation of his father, a respected though humble farmer, no passing reference to brothers or sisters of whom there were six, four older, two younger. There are none of the pleasantly insignificant anecdotes of childhood, no references to little fêtes or prize-winnings or of a scholarship, obtained through the interest of the village priest, which took the young Pétain to the Jesuit college at nearby St. Omer, none of the pleasant trivia that usually dot like daisies the recorded early years of famous old men.

And yet there is no disgrace concealed in these early years. Only an absence of splendor, an average of poverty, which marks the Marshal as kin to a majority of us.

The story is still meager when it reaches those frustrated and lonely years between twenty and sixty. For this is a life which began at an age when most lives are near their end. It is a life of contradiction, of luxury pursued for the sake of ambition, and of ambition constantly frustrated, in part by the inanimate perversity of events, in part by the narrow obstinacy of convictions not strong enough to elevate their possessor to martyrdom, not weak enough to be abandoned entirely to the dictates of expediency.

Philippe Pétain was a handsome and intelligent youth, a gifted student, a prepossessing companion. This much was evident to his companions at Saint-Cyr, where life was not easy for the poor and timid, since the most pampered and socially arbitrary youth of France sought admission there as aspiring cadets. But Pétain succeeded, by intelligence, by athletic superiority and by a diffident charm of manner, in effecting an entire detachment from Cauchy-la-Tour and in winning for himself pleasant invitations to the châteaux and villas of his companions.

This attractive and modestly eager young man had already shown himself adept at weighing the imponderable values of association, was already wise in keeping his own counsel and in dropping discreetly influences and relationships which could offer no future advantage. It was only natural that such a youth would early weigh the relative values of all available avenues to success. Most of his associates leaped at the chances offered by colonial service. A volunteer for such service could obtain double credit for each year spent abroad and would win a supplementary year for each campaign in which he served. This is why most of the great French generals of this period gained their experience and their stars in colonial warfare. The life was hard and uncomfortable, there was little social or political distraction, but promotion was quick and easy to obtain. Thus nine out of every ten ambitious young graduates chose this short cut to glory. Gallieni, Joffre, Lyautey, the conquerors of Madagascar; Gouraud, Mangin, Marchand, all were colonial generals. And the popularity of this swift route to promotion, incidentally, brought danger to France in later years, for all of these brilliant young apostles of the offensive had gained their experience against raw and unarmed natives whom they had subjugated with a minimum of trained manpower and modern weapons. The result was a mentality that in 1914 never once thought of the tragic absurdity of sending French troops charging against the might of the German Army as though it were the rabble of a petty native chieftain, certain to fall back in alarm at the sight of fixed bayonets.

Pétain considered the pros and cons of colonial service and decided against it. He was by now a recognized figure among the personable young lieutenants who paid court to the pretty heroines of country houseparties. In his always rather bleak fashion he was enjoying the easy gaiety, the charming frivolities of the sort of life open to well-mannered young officers, a society which would freeze without thinking the social aspirations of a strange young lawyer or a physician, or of an equally prepossessing young civil servant, but which was ready to accept at face value the dashing graduates of the military schools, even when their social standing was equal to, or lower than, that of the despised civilian.

Furthermore, the tremendous political repercussions of the War of 1870, the abortive coup of Marshal de MacMahon and the romantic tragedy, so nearly a triumph, of General Boulanger (that brave and adored hero who disappointed innumerable partisans, when their arrangements for his seizure of power were complete, by traveling instead to Brussels and there blowing out his brains upon the grave of his dead sweetheart) cannot have failed to affect the thinking of a young man of quick perception. Pétain debated the possibilities of military success far from political action and the alternate possibilities of the political influence open to officers of the French Army. He decided to stay at home, to pursue his career quietly, continuing polite attentions to the rich and powerful and keeping a steady eye upon the various avenues of military-political advancement.

He went purposefully to work. His excellent record made it easy for him to obtain admission to L'Ecole Supérieure de Guerre, that picked assemblage of the most studious and intelligent of all young French military men, from among whom were chosen, in due time, the officers of the General

Staff. These fortunate ones, saved from drying up their youth in the interminable maneuvers of small and dusty garrison towns, were the aides of the highest ranking generals, able to attract the favorable notice of the great ones by their unobtrusive tact, by the right word spoken at the right moment. Pétain was graduated with honors, and a place was found for him upon the staff of the military governor of Paris.

And then came the first of the great events which was to upset the calculations of the young man from Cauchy-la-Tour. L'Affaire Dreyfus was much more important in its implications and its after-effects than was the career at that time of one insignificant young soldier. Nevertheless, its effects upon that career were profound and incalculable. Between the War of 1870 and the Dreyfus scandal, Republican sentiment had been deemed tasteless and absurd by the smart young officers of the Army of France. A fashionable Catholicism was the vogue, and this must be sharply distinguished from the simple piety of the common Frenchman. In its essence it had far more in common with the callous opportunism of the Spanish aristocrats who united behind Franco in history's bloodiest civil war than it did with the humble religion of the village curé and his flock. It was fashionable to be seen at Mass, but it was not at all disgraceful to make adulterous assignations for the leisure hours which followed.

As a group, this rather loosely knit aggregation of the fashionable, the powerful, the imitative and the ambitious threw its considerable power behind the forces of reaction. And upon it the repercussions of the Dreyfus case were immediate and far-reaching. The case itself was a violent shock to the easygoing people of France, who had enjoyed the peaceful interval which followed the alarms and excursions of the MacMahon and Boulanger episodes. But here was an entrenched conspiracy, to maintain which officers, even generals, of the French Army committed perjury to keep an innocent man in prison merely because they wished to protect each other reciprocally from the consequences of a lie which set in motion an entire series of dastardly acts. This dangerous determination to involve the honor of the army with the honor of individual officers continued even after Colonel Henry, head of the famous Deuxième Bureau, committed suicide after leaving a confession of forgery. At last the nation understood that vague dreams of the retaking of Alsace and Lorraine through the efforts of these men, lost as they were in an ugly fog of moral confusion, had better be preceded by a thorough housecleaning. Without any definite announcement it was made clear that henceforth the officers marked for promotion would be those whose Republican sentiments were established beyond reproach.

This struck considerable confusion into the group so loosely and so inaccurately referred to as the Catholic Party. Prudent young men immediately began to deem it tactless to appear in uniform at Mass or to be seen associating too closely with prominent members of the group. For, to the lasting detriment of the true Catholic Church in France, and to the deeply felt religious convictions of Frenchmen everywhere, the fashionable churchgoers and active political mischief-makers, whose sentiments were consistently anti-democratic and bitterly reactionary, immediately and openly identified themselves with the persecutors of Captain Dreyfus. By doing so they compromised the entire Church and the multitude of its patient and God-fearing adherents in France. For the anti-clerical party, hitherto a small and unimportant minority group, was powerfully reinforced as a consequence by the large class of people who, in any democratic society, never take political sides until their anger or their sympathy is aroused. Its new and challenging leaders were men of the force of Jaurès, Clemenceau, Zola, Anatole France.

The ultimate result was that all liberal political elements aligned themselves with the anticlerical party without ever becoming in any sense the enemies of religion, while, with arrogant persistence, the reactionary elements continued to identify themselves with the Church without ever manifesting any of the unmistakable signs of Christian humility.

The two governments which followed the Dreyfus upheaval responded to popular pressure by inaugurating legislation for the separation of Church and State. The Republic decided that religious orders should no longer enjoy immunity from taxes on their large hereditary holdings. The piled-up riches of fifteen centuries held in the names of churches and monasteries were henceforth to be subject to the same taxes as the assets of ordinary corporations. Furthermore, a specific law obliged these congregations to declare the amount of their holdings. Many refused to do so, preferring to leave France. Others opposed the law with a passive resistance of such proportions that the government ordered inventories to be made in spite of them. This inspired bitter resentment in many an old curé and his parishioners, who were for the most part entirely incapable of understanding the conflicting forces which now were at work to destroy the peace of their ordered little world. Here and there throughout France the doors of churches and convents were barricaded against the secular officials by hysterical crowds of worshipers, composed largely of elderly women vaguely envisioning martyrs' crowns. Troops were ordered to force these doors and to push aside, humanely but firmly, their human barricades.

There has been some debate upon the extent and the sin-

cerity of Pétain's Catholicism—as to how much it is a genuine
piety, remaining intact from those far-off years at Cauchy-la-
Tour and how much the affectation of a nature which found
its most congenial company among the people who instinctively affiliated themselves, without any deep conviction, with
the natural authoritarianism of the Church. In this respect
as in so many others, he no doubt has been both sincere and
opportunistic. As with so many men of his period and type,
Pétain has been able both to divorce religion from life, when
it suited him, and to make it the excuse for some of his most
inexplicably ruthless actions, also when it suited him. Religion
did not deter him from enjoying the frivolities so freely available in his youth, nor from following the common practice
among impoverished young officers of his time and class of
substituting discreet, and much less expensive, flirtations with
discontented young matrons for the holy matrimony which
the Church urges upon her children. In this respect he was
neither worse nor better than his fellows, and it is only in the
light of his recent reproaches to the French nation that his
record becomes a matter for comment.

In the matter of Church versus State which faced him at
the turn of the century, it is probable that a man of similar
but deeper conviction than Pétain would have refused to carry
out the orders extended to him. Other officers did, and it is
unlikely that the financial sacrifice entailed in thus subordinat-
ing career to conviction would have been of long duration.
Major Pétain had not cultivated his friendships for nothing,
and for a young man who would abandon his career in such
a cause much might have been arranged.

But he, and others like him, taught by nothing in their
education or surroundings to understand or respect the democratic processes of government, obeyed their orders while

making no secret of their repugnance. And the experience, for Pétain, turned what had been a mild, half-amused contempt for the Republic into a scarcely concealed hostility. It became fashionable now to refer to Marianne, that half-rowdy, half-affectionate, wholly undignified personification of the Third Republic, as "the Slut."

Pétain's estrangement from the Republic was not lessened as the conviction forced itself home that henceforth preferment would be progressively difficult for the officer with clerical leanings, would be made easy only for the aggressive Republican, the man whose political convictions could be proclaimed from the housetops without affronting a newly sensitive populace. He was at this time professor of tactics at the same deservedly proud Ecole Supérieure de Guerre. Here he had not made his own path of advancement any less rough by opposing to the theories of offensive warfare brilliantly expounded by the college's dean, General Foch, his own meticulously worked-out beliefs upon the merits of a strategy of defense. Here again the conflict between Pétain's obstinacy and his ambition is curiously demonstrated. A purely opportunistic nature would have abandoned the less popular theory once he had understood that it would be unlikely to aid in the upward climb. But Pétain throughout his long life has been a passionate believer in defensive war and in the negative virtues of passivity. He gave no ground to General Foch, and his jealous dislike of this brilliant, generous and impulsive man apparently dates all the way back to this original difference. Pétain, like most of the "Gars de ch'nord" as the men of his cold and damp region have nicknamed themselves, is easily angered and implacable when once his dislike has been aroused.

He became at this time a lieutenant colonel. He knew that

promotion beyond the rank of colonel was unlikely, that his further advancement at the college was more so. Still extremely handsome, he was also a popular if cautious bachelor, an intelligent, sensitive and increasingly disappointed man. But particularly he was an increasingly disappointed soldier. On every hand men of lesser intellect, poorer training, men who had never watched for the knock of opportunity with his single-minded caution, were happily assured of advancement. After the turmoils and intrigues of decades, the Republic was determined to entrust its future military destinies neither to geniuses nor demagogues but to safe and kindly men, inspired bookkeepers in whom the worm of ambition seldom stirred—and then in no vital part.

And so the man who had planned for a great career was nearing sixty with the possibilities of that career narrowing themselves to vanishing point. Among the people he had counted upon to help his rise he was still a popular and sought-after figure. But these wealthy conservatives, contemptuous of the type of politician now firmly entrenched within the Republic, were scarcely the sort of people whom the soldier of that era of reform could regard as assets. In luxurious seclusion they held aloof, entertaining their friends and themselves, and delighted with the continued company of the distinguished lieutenant colonel.

For it was not at all a disagreeable or a self-denying life to which this solitary being was now condemned. He lived among idle and self-indulgent people who were almost totally cynical where sexual morality was concerned. Although divorce was severely frowned upon, illicit love was a normal social convenience. The woman honest enough to seek a divorce had procured a one-way ticket to disrepute and would no longer be welcomed in the drawing rooms of even her dearest friends. But the same woman, accompanied by a lover and her indifferent or complaisant husband, was accepted as a matter of course, and it would be a strangely gauche or neglectful hostess who did not keep up with the current extra marital loves of her guests and arrange their accommodations accordingly. One of the commonplace sights of this era was the trio composed of Anatole France, his well-known and well-born mistress and her equally well-known husband. In perfect amity they traveled everywhere together and accepted all invitations à trois.

In this society the handsome bachelor, Colonel Pétain, was neither more nor less conventional than his companions. Such mention of his personal life is stressed here only because the lady to whom at this time he reputedly gave the most single-hearted devotion of his career was a lovely and gentle Jewish woman. Apparently her influence only suspended, but did not cure, the latent anti-Semitism which from time to time has marked the Marshal's whole life and which culminated in 1940 in the ugly and repressive laws against Jews which marked one more affront to the stricken spirit of France.

Such was Pétain's career, its most vital aspects seemingly near their close, a few years before the first World War. He was now assistant dean at the Advanced School of Military Cavalry at Saumur. This, the most fashionable branch of military service, attracted pupils from the very society in which the Marshal felt himself most at home. He was now invited as a matter of course to the most exclusive houses in France, to those of the conservative bankers, the wealthy and powerful manufacturers with whom he was never entirely to lose touch again during the exciting years ahead. Among this fairly small circle of friends and acquaintances he was an impressive and potentially useful figure. In the military world, the world he had chosen for his own, he was a failure. Further promotion was quite unlikely, and there remained in view, after a few more years of instructing the young and flattering their elders, only the drab prospects of retirement on a colonel's pension and the long, quiet years of brooding until the end. It would seem, now, that the young men who had flocked to the colonies had chosen more wisely. They were generals and could boast of their decorations. The tangible rewards of the salons and the boudoirs somehow had not materialized, and the chances for political influence upon the men of this cruder and tougher manifestation of the Third Republic were rather slim for quiet and contemptuous colonels who chose their friends among the aristocracies of birth and wealth.

Of the man himself at this period we have an odd and revealing picture. It is the vouched-for anecdote of one of his contemporaries and former comrades.

Four years before the outbreak of war Pétain was named to the command of the 33rd Infantry Regiment at Arras. Arriving there, he was met by the lieutenant colonel, a man who had been in his class at Saint-Cyr and had there for some months been his best friend and roommate. This subordinate came forward with hands outstretched, enthusiastic in his welcome, and addressed his old friend in a torrent of inquiries as *tu*, the second person singular mode of address which in France denotes affectionate familiarity. The reply from Pétain was an icy shower.

"Colonel," he interrupted. "I must request you to keep your distance. I shall require you to salute me, to speak to me only as *vous* [the formal, second person plural] and, when you must address me, I should prefer to be called '*mon colonel*'." [This is the extremely formal mode of address from a subordinate to a superior, equivalent to "sir."]

There was no relaxation of this barrier so suddenly erected before the baffled and disconcerted former friend. Actually the difference between a colonel and a lieutenant colonel is so slight as to be indistinguishable, particularly where old friendship exists. But in later months, when the regiment left for maneuvers, the two men had often to dine in the only restaurant in the village. Colonel Pétain consistently ate alone at a small table. Furthermore, since he had extended his prohibition of familiarity through all the commissioned ranks, his subordinate had to dine alone, with the remaining officers of the regiment occupying another separate table, and with a deathlike silence prevailing.

But, for the aging and frustrated regimental commander, fate had one last great chance in store, and during this same summer of maneuvers the Great War commenced.

CHAPTER 2

LIFE BEGINS AT SIXTY

I CAN WELL REMEMBER the amazement with which the more militarily alert members of my family met the news that Colonel Pétain had suddenly been made commander of the Second Army. I was home on my first furlough at the time and the reaction of my father and uncles was that there must be, incredible though it seemed, listed somewhere in the *Military Yearbook*—that *Who's Who* of the French Army— another Pétain. And, remembering the sedate and aging professor, I too marveled that a mere colonel of such modest attributes could, by some miracle, suddenly have leaped the interminable barriers to promotion, the dreary intermediary steps between his rank and the dizzying height of full general to which now, apparently, he had attained.

But it was the same Pétain. That colorless instructor of the new military generation, withering quietly upon the vine, was transformed into a young and seemingly brilliant commander. Never since the days of the Revolution had so astonishing a metamorphosis upset the staid procedures of French army promotions. And the story of how it all happened is long and rather involved.

When war broke out the High Command met it with a front of unshakable complacence. Everything was wonderful. The morale of the army was magnificent, from the youngest recruit to the topmost general. Equipment was plentiful, completely modern and able to compete with anything the enemy had to offer. All that remained was to sail confidently into battle, retake the lost provinces with a flurry of drums, obliterate the disaster of 1871 and teach the brash Germans a lesson.

The disillusion that followed was complete and devastating. Equipment proved to be totally inadequate. The hierarchy of generals was steeped in the virtues of offensive warfare—and indeed one who had been so rash as to suggest to the High Command the possibility of a defensive war would have been regarded with a suspicious dismay. This offense was entrusted to a group of generals who had always declared that infantry was queen of the battlefield and that the bayonet, that most useful of weapons, was the answer to any and every situation encountered in war. This belief is not of itself dangerous. Indeed we have recently seen how magnificently it can succeed. The tragedy in 1914 was that the French generals believed this without ever relating it to the size and quality and the offensive training of the armies themselves. In addition, the French intelligence service, the Deuxième Bureau, had lamentably failed in its task of reporting German progress in armaments development and manufacture.

So it is not remarkable that the campaign began badly. Generalissimo Joffre knew nothing of the dispositions made by the enemy. He concluded that the march across Belgium was merely a feint and that large masses of the German forces would be found waiting across the Rhine. So the French armies advanced, meeting no opposition, and swiftly occupied Altkirch in Alsace. On the following day, August 9, Mulhouse was taken, and on the tenth it was lost, to be recaptured once again by General Pau. On the twelfth another French

army attacked in Lorraine and here the Germans were awaiting them, in positions previously and thoroughly prepared.
Casualties were immediate and heavy as the French, terribly
visible in the gay red trousers of which they were so pathetically proud, advanced à la baïonette. The battle was a costly
and humiliating lesson. The cadets of Saint-Cyr had kept
the pledge they had made on their graduation just two weeks
earlier. As serious, fledgling young second lieutenants they had
charged at the heads of their platoons in the bright blue,
red and white uniforms of the Academy, complete even to
white gloves and the famous shako with its tossing panache
of tricolored ostrich feathers. The result was massacre; and
in their loss and that of the troops which followed them,
the army of elderly theoreticians learned the dangers and
the uses of barbed wire, machine-gun nests, heavy howitzers
and uniforms which become protectively invisible in the
monotone of a trench.

And so the swiftly and too easily reconquered Alsace and
Lorraine were as swiftly and more expensively lost again.
The offensive spirit, unsupported as it was by offensive
matériel, had received a crushing blow. The General Staff
rather belatedly permitted itself to wonder whether offense
without the wherewithal to be offensive was worth the heavy
cost in life. And, since heavy cannon and machine guns now
had hurriedly to be manufactured, they wondered whether,
in the long waiting period, it might not be more prudent to
spare as much as possible their human cannon fodder.

It was then that these chagrined gentlemen recalled the
existence of Colonel Pétain, this quiet and rather dull little
teacher who, amid the staid proprieties of routine classroom
procedures, had nevertheless dared to preach the heretical
values of defense. Alone he had maintained the value of

defensive war, of the quiet and well-prepared wait at well-chosen positions and the superior virtues of the counterattack when the attacker had spent his strength. It was decided to test the exponent of so useful a theory and so the colonel was given a brigade. Not yet, however, was he given also the title of brigadier. This had to be earned.

Meanwhile the French armies of the northeast had entered Belgium to proceed to the rescue of King Albert and the hard-pressed Belgian Army. The Flemish battlefields have never been propitious for France, and 1940 was only the last of a long series of tragedies to be enacted upon those vast flat plains which had seen the defeats of Agincourt, Waterloo and Charleroi. Nevertheless, few generals have resisted the temptation to be drawn once again onto that vast emptiness where the massed troops look so imposing and are killed with such ease.

Since the defeat at Morhange the French General Staff had thought with dismay of any such battle of masses. But it was now too late to change plans. It would take months to convert the army from its target-bright plumage to uniforms of horizon blue, and years to supply the number of machine guns necessary to equip such a force. Indeed the quality of the guns was as much of a problem as their quantity and the author can well remember coming across his companion fliers in the early days of air warfare actually weeping with rage and frustration because the machine guns in their planes would jam regularly at the beginning of each fight, making escape with life, let alone victory, a matter of precarious luck.

And so the troops which gathered upon the plain of Charleroi found themselves facing an enemy well supplied with every modern weapon while they lacked everything that could equalize the struggle. Howitzers were few and inferior in quality; ammunition was never received on time or in sufficient quantities. Only by the exercise of a sheer, naked bravery heartbreaking in its implications and its later results did the French *poilus* neutralize the disaster awaiting them at Charleroi. They fled to the Marne at such whirlwind speed that the Germans, unpracticed then in the blitz techniques, could not possibly follow without abandoning their heavy guns and the cumbersome munitions supplies. By their headlong dash the French purchased a brief advantage in time and even a temporary equality in matériel and thus were able to veer around and snatch a victory from their rout.

The adventure cost France almost half of her active army. But again it had taught valuable lessons. When the cost was counted the dull and correctly Republican generals seemed at a considerable disadvantage. Only the elderly theoretician had emerged with anything resembling glory, and of all the brigades it seemed that the one entrusted to Colonel Pétain had best known how to adapt itself to the German technique of counterattack on prepared terrain. And this was because the German General Staff had applied, with all its tremendous material resources, the very theories expounded for years in the classrooms and textbooks of Pétain.

After Charleroi, Joffre was given a free hand. Politically irreproachable generals were tumbled from their posts, and the way was wide open for men of ability to rise to new heights, provided only that their theories of war could stand the test of battle conditions. The result was that Pétain, who was not even a brigadier general at the start, emerged from the Battle of the Marne a major general; and immediately afterward he was given command of an army corps.

Thus, in six weeks there rose to glory this morose and introspective man whom the war's beginning apparently had left high and dry, passed over in his professorial cold storage for men who were his inferiors in tactical knowledge. So swift had been his elevation that the new corps commander had to greet his own staff of generals in the old uniform of a colonel in which he had come to war. Pétain has never been a man of enthusiasms, of warm and quick responses. Nevertheless he did, at this time, begin to warm himself cautiously at the unaccustomed glow of public acclaim, and the warmth was good to a starved soul. But the thaw that pervaded this bleak personality was controlled and circumspect. Its influence extended perhaps to Joffre, who had recognized him, and to the subordinates who now attended his words with wide eyes and respectful assents, but it never spread to encompass the politicians who had scorned him nor to the ambitious soldiers who were potentially his rivals.

Now the wintry sunshine of his success was to reach its zenith. The spring of 1915 brought the offensive in Artois, the region from which he came, and every hedge and stick of which he seemed to know by heart. Lieutenant General Pétain was able to show himself here as good a commander in offensive campaign as he was in the varied strategies of defense. No detail was too small for his personal attention. The careless error, the unexpected hitch, never appeared to mar the plans of Pétain. Patiently, methodically he worked out the possibilities of error and surprise ahead of time and duly provided for every eventuality. In June of that year he handed over command of the 33rd Army Corps to General Fayolle—later a Marshal of France—and took charge of the Second Army as a full-ranking general. In September he commanded the Champagne offensive, undertaking personally a task of preparation requiring almost superhuman patience and attention. Not a single gun battery escaped his visit. Every officer was personally instructed in his objectives, questioned as to his understanding.

At this time Pétain turned his meticulous attention to a problem hitherto insoluble. It had been the constant complaint of the infantry that the artillery supposed to support it in attack fired only according to a blind schedule which automatically advanced the range, never knowing whether the unfortunate infantrymen were either in advance or behind on their schedule. As a result there were always a number of dead and wounded victims of the supporting artillery fire. Pétain cured this by inventing a large white board which, carried by the attacking troops and kept well within sight of the supporting lines, marked accurately the progress or retreat of the infantry. This ingenious device plus the phenomenal correctness of range of the famous French 75, produced the sight of shells falling with precision around troops in motion, with the gun range lengthening or shortening itself apparently by magic. It was one of the few complete surprises of warfare the French were able to give the German armies in that campaign.

This and other evidences of his tireless attention to detail tremendously endeared Pétain to the rank and file of his troops, who were envied by the men of the other armies. Among his equals—already there were not so many—he was at this time, if not always liked, certainly very much admired, and this applied, for a time at least, even to his old superior, General Foch, now merely the equal of his former subordinate and forced to regard the defensive theories over which he had smiled with a mild irritation in the past as the serious contenders to his own doctrines of the offensive. Foch had not actually been proved wrong by Pétain. He had merely, as had most of his colleagues, been too easygoing to envision the material needs necessary to the success of his plans. And now the pendulum had swung in the other direction. Former worshipers of the offensive, dashingly conceived, essentially nebulous in outline, now were marveling at the success of the defensive campaign, buttressed by hitherto unheard-of attention to detail.

Joffre, modest, imperturbable, beloved, followed in silence this lightning progress of Pétain, who had now attained the status of France's youngest army commander. The greatest merit of this calm and wise old man lay in his capacity for listening. He sought the advice of equal and subordinate alike, listened gravely and chose his plan from among the multitude of suggestions thus developed. It may be true that he lacked any capacity for developing his own ideas but, once convinced of the merit of any suggestion, he would make it his by adoption, work out its details and assume all responsibility for success or lack of it.

The Battle of the Marne had long been a grief and a frustration to Joffre, and debate long and sometimes acrimonious has raged around whose should be the credit for final victory, his or Marshal Gallieni's. It is certain that the daring plan of throwing against the moving right wing of General von Kluck the army of General Maunoury, who according to all the rulebooks of war should have been preoccupied with the defense of Paris, was a suggestion made by Gallieni to Joffre. But it was Joffre who, after study, weighing and eventual acceptance, took all the responsibility for a plan far too audacious to have occurred even to the cool and daring heads of the German General Staff. Joffre himself answered this question as to who was the victor of the Marne with a wistful little comment. To an English newspaperman who put the question bluntly to him he answered rather slowly,

"Nobody seems willing to grant that I won the Battle of the Marne. But everybody would be agreed that the responsibility was all mine had I lost it."

This human and philosophic old man had as his right hand the strange and dashingly named General de Curières de Castelnau whose nickname among his subordinates was *Capucin Botté* [Monk in Boots]. Joffre was a Freemason and a Republican. General de Castelnau was passionately Catholic. And, agreeing on no other subject in the world, these two were utterly at one in their selfless patriotism and their absolutely impartial sense of justice where the prosecution of the war was concerned. Thus with these two men Pétain was assured of a fair and generous consideration of his plans and his successes. In addition to this he was successful in winning the respect if not the affection of Joffre, who always had had a reverence for details and who was favorably impressed by the officers who watched them. General Joffre belonged to the Engineer Corps and throughout his career the physical realities of bridges, pontoons, fortifications and roads continued to fascinate him. In Pétain he met for the first time an infantry officer who yet succeeded in thinking like an engineer. But it was his passion for detail that completely won the generalissimo. If General Pétain said that ten hours were necessary to undertake a certain maneuver, then ten hours turned out to be just about the right length of time. And there were none of the stock excuses for delay forthcoming either, since the road that might be overcrowded or the railway junction that might be blocked had always been considered by the meticulous Pétain.

Thus Pétain embarked upon that winter of 1915-16 a comparatively happy and satisfied man, secure in the approval

of his superiors, the admiring envy of his equals and subordinates. So far nothing had occurred to arouse that latent
tendency toward resentment, later so noticeable, or to irritate
the exposed sensibilities of the man who still had much of
failure to forget. And he had not made the mistake of others
who had channeled their resentment against a lack of reinforcements into a fierce condemnation of the British for their
slowness in recruiting and equipping troops. There was something to be said in extenuation of this viewpoint. When war
broke out England was able to put only two hundred thousand trained and equipped troops into battle, while the
French, who had conscription, mobilized five million men
in one month. French casualties at the Battle of Charleroi
alone exceeded the number of British troops available in the
first winter of war, and it was not until the winter of 1915
that a million Tommies were mobilized. It took another year
to prepare the second million and conscription was intro-
duced only in 1916, while the total mobilization of seven
million troops was not reached until 1918. The British themselves were severe enough critics of the early delays and
muddles of the Asquith government, and there was no tendency on their part to minimize the need for swifter and more
efficient action. Nevertheless the French, who felt that for
almost two years they had borne the major burden almost
alone, were occasionally sharp in criticism, although such
sharpness was never discernible in the topmost military and
political circles, which understood, perhaps better than their
underlings, some of the difficulties with which the British had
to contend in their effort to swing a nation geared to the
leisures of peace into the hustle of war.

The winter of 1915–16 was alert with the plans for a
tremendous joint offensive along the Somme. But alas for the

planners, and their intelligence officers. The Germans also had been planning and their plan for Verdun was ready first. Furthermore it was a masterpiece of surprise and of the then fledgling art of camouflage. For weeks beforehand quiet and boredom ruled the entire sector during daylight hours. But the moment darkness fell, thousands of troops poured silently in, batteries were soundlessly set in place and as soundlessly hidden from view, millions of shells were concealed in the surrounding woods.

General Balfourier, commanding the army of Verdun, remained in complete ignorance of all this stealthy preparation. The first attack, on February 21, 1916, was a complete and appalling surprise. His army faltered under the impact and it began to look as though Allied public opinion, vaguely hopeful at the thought of vigorous offensive action to come with the spring, must be greeted instead with the unforeseen catastrophe of the loss of Verdun.

General de Castelnau hurried to the new front, armed with full powers. And then began the series of events which was both to make and mar the future career of General Pétain. At this moment he was a popular hero, surrounded by the sort of glamor with which modern children have enveloped Superman. And on the fourth day of the German onslaught the army of Verdun found new life and courage in the news that General Pétain had replaced Balfourier. And indeed a task fit for Superman faced the new commander. The enemy had managed in this short space to capture the zone, four miles in depth, which housed most of the vital and irreplaceable strategic artillery positions. This penetration made defense of the fortified city a task of appalling difficulty and expense.

The story of Verdun up to this point illustrates, as many

similar instances in the present war have done, the tragic mistakes that can be committed by military commanders who abide by all the rules but who lack imagination. General Balfourier and his subordinate, General Herr, had left the key position, the fortress of Douaumont, under the care of less than a company of second reserve troops, without precise orders and almost without arms! This was because they could not imagine the Germans daring to attack Douaumont without a previous artillery shelling of several days, a warning which would give the French ample time to man and arm the fortress.*

But General Balfourier is not wholly to be blamed. To him and to his superiors an advance of three hundred feet in a day was considered a victory. An advance of four miles in a day was scarcely within the scope of possibility, let alone of probability, and thus the fortress of Douaumont, four miles from the point of attack, was considered to be well out of immediate danger.

Pétain himself, in his own description of the Battle of Verdun, has given an interesting account of the capture of Douaumont. A German captain, at the head of a lost patrol far out of touch with its own lines, suddenly saw the fortress lowering upon him from a distance of less than five hundred yards, seemingly bristling with machine guns and cannon. He heard the alert sounded by French sentries. Glancing around, he saw not the slightest chance for successful flight and, resenting the tameness of surrender, he ordered his men to storm the fortress and die as heroes. They did so and, to their joyful amazement, this most famous of French fortifications

---

* For an almost identical example of lack of vision, the reader is referred to Daniel Vilfroy's eyewitness account of the Battle of France, War in the West, which describes the consequences of the French General Staff's careless reliance upon the "impenetrable" Ardennes Forest in the defense of Sedan.

quietly submitted to them. There was not even enough defensive strength to hold it against a handful of lost Germans.

But a change was impending and the new commander had a dramatic opportunity to show his mettle. To the German press and public the fall of Verdun was a foregone conclusion. Announcements of the smashing victory already were locked in special edition forms of the Berlin newspapers, awaiting only the signal to be rushed through the presses and into the hands of the hopefully waiting populace. High in a near-by lookout, the Kaiser himself gazed upon the entrenched camp of Verdun through field glasses and waited to see his confident troops administer the *coup de grâce*.

Twenty-four hours later the Emperor had left, the special editions were being quietly dismembered by newspaper staffs. General Pétain's counterattack had succeeded in driving back the enemy across almost all the lost ground, and the defensive positions before Verdun were cleared for French troops.

But the city was not saved. For months following, the German armies attacked with relentless force and skill. The roads and railways in their possession, fifteen in all, made possible almost limitless supplies of munitions. They were able to fire an average of one hundred thousand shells a day while the French were never able to use more than eleven thousand in the same length of time. The fact was that Verdun, three parts surrounded, had to depend for supplies upon one secondary highway, that of Bar-le-Duc, and the narrow-gauge railway line known as the Meusien.

And now Pétain's talent for organization showed itself at its inspired best. He used the methods of a Henry Kaiser to keep his one poor road in condition. The heavy tires of the trucks of that period tore it daily to pieces and daily Pétain rebuilt it. Three eight-hour shifts of eight thousand laborers did nothing else for months but repair the road. There was neither time nor truck space to transport the stone needed, and so quarries were opened in the surrounding hills. In this way the road remained open during the entire siege, and seven thousand trucks a day were dedicated to carrying fifty thousand men and ninety thousand tons of munitions a week to the battlefield.

The story of Verdun is too well known to need repetition here. Slowly and at terrible cost the lost terrain was reconquered and the long agony was at last a French victory. And the cost was literally terrible, to both attackers and defenders. A total of three hundred and fifty thousand Frenchmen was sacrificed to this victory and the story of the Chasseurs Alpins was repeated with many different actors in the role of victim. Two battalions of this regiment of Alpine rangers, commanded by Colonel Driant, held the woods of Caures for two days against an entire enemy division. By the evening of the second day this force of twelve hundred was reduced to a hundred and ten, and the colonel and all his officers had been killed.

But the effect of Verdun upon Pétain—and upon France—was profound. To the French people he emerged an almost sanctified figure, larger and more awful than life, the contriver of a victory torn from the very heart and nerves of France herself. To the leaders of France, political and military, he had become a problem with profoundly discouraging implications. The mounting costs of Verdun soon became an unending nightmare to these men. Pétain was insatiable in his demand for reinforcements. To have pleased him wholly, almost every man under arms in France would sooner or later have had to be earmarked for this blood bath. To Joffre it was impossible that such demands should be met. France could not stand or fall upon Verdun. There was the Somme offensive, upon which the English were counting heavily. Their protests helped strengthen Joffre's determination not to sacrifice this carefully laid plan to the crucible of Verdun. Nevertheless Joffre succeeded merely in producing discontent on both sides. He sent some of the Somme troops to Pétain, thus disrupting a part of the Anglo-French schedule. But he did not send enough to pacify the omnivorous Pétain. The result was that the long-looked-for Somme offensive was not outstandingly successful, and the Battle of Verdun was won at a cost appalling to contemplate.

Actually Pétain did not stay with the siege of Verdun until its bitter end. His subordinate, General Nivelle, took final command and it was the opinion of General Joffre* that it was General Nivelle who snatched victory from an almost certain defeat. "If history accords me the right to judge those generals who served under me," he declares, "then in justice I must say that the true hero of Verdun was Nivelle, with the aid of Mangin." To Pétain, Joffre gives credit for having brought order out of disorganization. But he casts a strange light upon this seemingly indomitable commander.

"Repeatedly," he says, "I urged upon General Pétain the need of striking back. I pointed out to him how dangerous our situation would be if we never recovered, however little by little, the ground we had lost." He describes the "exaggerated importance" Pétain attached to Verdun, saying that had his demands been granted "the entire French Army would have been absorbed."

The "pessimism" of Marshal Pétain, so marked in the concluding days of the Battle of France in 1940 and throughout the following armistice negotiations, has been spoken of by

* *Mémoirs*, Volume II.

his apologists as one of the inevitable results of old age and of the cruel shocks of 1940. It is interesting to note the number of references to this pessimism, strong enough to be remarkable even to the leaders of twenty-seven years ago. Marshal Joffre remarks more than once in his *Mémoirs* upon the extreme pessimism of Pétain. He "once more scared everybody," Joffre says at one point. "His confidence in the length of time Verdun could hold out was so limited that he even went so far as to tell Castelnau that it could stand for no more than another eight days."

This pessimism, so outstanding a feature of Pétain's mental outlook, undoubtedly was a major factor in his having been passed over at the time of Joffre's replacement. For public shock and dismay over the losses of 1916 demanded a scapegoat and it was Papa Joffre, apostle of the war of attrition, who must go. To the people it seemed that the side upon which attrition was doing its deadly work was their own and they could not see that the German armies had suffered much from the policies of Joffre.

To the lonely and arrogant, but withal unsure, mind of Pétain, which claimed, as the public generously accorded, full credit for the victory of Verdun, notwithstanding the last-minute efforts of General Nivelle, it seemed almost a foregone conclusion that he should replace the old generalissimo. Joffre's opinion of him is one of the reasons why the choice did not fall upon him. Others may be found in the even franker misgivings of Poincaré and Clemenceau, recorded at a later date in the war. Raymond Poincaré quotes Clemenceau in 1918 as reporting that he had had to reproach Pétain for "exaggerated pessimism."

"He told me," Clemenceau is quoted as saying, "that if we are defeated, the British will be to blame." On another occasion Poincaré reports that Clemenceau told him, in some distress, of Pétain's opinion that "the Germans will beat the British in open country and after that they will defeat us too."

"Should a general speak, or even think, like that?" Clemenceau wanted to know.

Several observers have testified that in the discouraged March of 1918 it was Pétain's firm opinion that an armistice was the only hope for France. A prophetic declaration.

Poincaré also quotes both the cruelest and the kindest estimates of Pétain given at that time by his former and his then present commander-in-chief. Said Joffre: "Both Pétain and Anthoine [another French general] lack character." Foch, when, two years later, he had been promoted to Marshal over the head of Pétain, told Poincaré that "on a secondary level, as a craftsman, Pétain is perfect, but he quails before responsibility and could not act as commander-in-chief."

Nevertheless, in spite of his not being chosen for this great honor, Pétain had won, in 1916, glory enough to have satisfied a more generous spirit and to have reconciled him with the "politicians" upon whom he blamed most of his earlier lack of progress. He was one of the three foremost military chieftains and the wearer of the Grand Cross of the Legion of Honor. But it was a bitter blow that General Nivelle, who had come at the eleventh hour to receive the honors of the victory of Verdun, should also become the generalissimo who replaced Joffre. And it is true that the appointment was not a fortunate one, although both Joffre and Poincaré had, they felt, good grounds for not entrusting the post to so gloomy and so easily discouraged a commander as Pétain. They could not forget the number of times Pétain had longed to abandon Verdun, his reluctance amounting at times almost to defiance, to take any positive action which might shorten the long

agony. He had held out, in fact, only upon the categoric
orders of Joffre, who had demanded that the spot be held
until the Somme offensive could relieve pressure upon the
sector. "If you can't hold them with the support of our
strongest fortification," Joffre asked him, "how do you think
you can stop them in the open country?"

Joffre, the conservative, whose slogan had been, for two
heartbreaking years, "I am whittling away at them," was
replaced by Nivelle the opportunist, one of the apostles of
the dashing offensive, and in May of 1917, Nivelle hurled
the French Army, helter-skelter, against the Germans in
Champagne.

The results were disastrous. The *poilu* had been willing to
die at Verdun because he had understood that there he must
hold fast, at whatever the cost. Furthermore he knew that
at the end Verdun had been a victory which he had helped
make. But in Champagne no such factors held. He had no
faith in the attack and correctly judged it to be an offensive
undertaken largely for the glory of a newly appointed generalissimo. The campaign failed, mutinies occurred in one
of the best-disciplined armies of Europe, whole regiments
refused to return to the trenches.

Nivelle departed, and the superseded Pétain, now almost
the last hope, replaced him. Again, in another type of man
the occasion would have produced something like satisfaction.
But to Pétain it was a continuance of the bitter fate which
called him always to rectify the mistakes of others, to attain
honor only because another had failed. Furthermore he felt
that he was being called upon by the politicians he despised
to save them from the error for which they alone were to
blame, the appointment of an incompetent general.

The appointment, while it pleased the public which had

already conceded Pétain full credit for Verdun, was not an ideal one, for the reasons already shown, either for the French army chiefs or for the Allies. Liddell Hart, the British military analyst, summed up the British reaction by commenting, "Indeed, he was the type of man whose services a democracy would only call on in a dark hour."

Nevertheless he was commander-in-chief at last. And fifteen months later, in the spring of 1918, the Allies had to face the question of a supreme command. Ludendorff, rid of the Russians, was concentrating all his forces against the Franco-British armies. He had succeeded in piercing their front, just at the junction near Montdidier. Almost instinctively Pétain decided. His armies would abandon the British and save Paris. The dilemma which drove Marshal Marmont to treason in 1814 and defeated Weygand in 1940 now arose to plague Pétain. The question was whether to preserve Paris at the risk of losing France or to save France at the risk of damage to Paris. To Pétain it was almost no question. Paris should be preserved at any cost, even if it meant deserting the British.

Logically Pétain was the choice for supreme commander. The Italian general, Cadorna, a brave and capable man, was out of the question as he himself agreed. Douglas Haig, the British general, had no disposition to press for command. His army was numerically smaller and the British were in command of the Anglo-French fleet. As for General Pershing, his armies were a small part of those in the field and he was as yet largely untried. Finally it was a matter of justice that the enormous losses and sacrifices sustained by the French entitled them to make final decisions where they were needed. So that Pétain, the French chief of staff, was the logical, indeed the only, man for the post.

But the British were not unmindful of Pétain's attitude

toward them. In the case of a debacle it would, they knew, be Pétain's army first and the devil take the hindmost. Not only did they share the general doubts and worries of his own leaders but they felt the added worry of a dislike the French commander scarcely troubled to conceal.

General Foch, once the chief's superior and now his subordinate, accompanied him to the conference called at Doullens to decide upon the supreme command. Before voting the Allied ministers present held an informal poll of the generals present: What did they think of the situation?

Pétain was positive. Only a new retreat could gain the necessary time. American reinforcements were arriving. The thing to do was to retreat, to wait for them, to mark time until they were ready. And in the meantime Ludendorff might, perhaps, get tired.

Foch was out of the competition. But he was never afraid to speak his mind. Furthermore his seniority and prestige assured him of a respectful hearing at any gathering of his peers. He erupted now into a frenzy.

"Retreat . . . always retreat! This is what results from that famous dogma of 'defensive at all costs!' How can one hope to win by losing all the battles? True the offensive did not succeed in the beginning. Let that be! It was because the Allies were insufficiently equipped, had at that time everything to build and create. Now we are as strong as the enemy. Only an offensive position can save the situation!"

Foch had his analysis ready and he hurled it. For years all attacks had been failing because of the same obstacles. Either there was an insufficient artillery barrage and the storming troops were stopped short by machine-gun nests, with the results a useless massacre, or the onslaught à la Pétain with the heavy pounding of gunfire destroying all obstacles within a small sector cost a fortune in shells to achieve the occupation of an empty waste of no man's land. And this last was because, Foch explained, the very intensity of the shelling informed the Germans that an attack was imminent and so they utilized the bombardment period to bring up all their reinforcements to the point of attack.

What was needed, continued Foch, was to attack upon one point after an artillery barrage, thus attracting enemy reserves, and then to stop purposely, after a limited advance. Then, without leaving the enemy time to draw breath, the maneuver should be repeated on another sector of the front. Thus the enemy would never know where to send his reserves; always they would arrive too late, when the attack was finished at that point and begun again upon some other part of the line.

"I attack them here, and here, and here," cried the furious little general. "I leave them breathless. I crush them. If you would only listen to me! . . ."

He was listened to, in silence. Then Lord Milner and Douglas Haig retired to a window recess and whispered together. They returned and said that the British Empire was ready to accept a supreme command under a French general, on condition that this general was their friend, General Foch.

Thus it was decided. And Pétain never forgave the British this slight, never forgot that it was they who took away from him the supreme honor, to give it to his old and constant rival. Conqueror of Verdun seemed a slight distinction indeed beside the glory that was Foch's. And when, following the Armistice, the former colonel-instructor was made a marshal of France, his prevailing emotion was a bitter disappointment that the honor followed by several months its bestowal on Marshal Foch.

CHAPTER 3

THE LEGACY OF FOCH

TWENTIETH-CENTURY HEADS of the French Republic had studied well both the history of France and the military mind. And what was true of the atmosphere of French officers' clubs probably is true of most aggregations of military men during the long doldrums of peace. Here conversation turned scarcely ever to tactics, strategy, equipment or morale, but to a surprising degree occupied itself with the details of seniority, annuities, promotions (just and unjust), age limits, and the extent and ramifications of political pull. The most popular reading matter was not the impressive collection of volumes on the art, science and fortunes of war, but the dull page of the *Journal Officiel* with its daily listing of promotions, and the *Military Yearbook*. And the one unfailing cause of passionate dispute was the occasional promotion of some fellow officer which proved to be inexplicable by the normal rules of seniority.

So long as an officer had a hope of higher rank he remained more or less amenable to the dictates of the Ministry of War. But the supreme rank, that of Marshal of France, automatically removed its possessor from any further competition for promotion and from the proddings of unsatisfied ambition. Those to whom it had in the past been accorded had shown themselves quick to acquire a dangerous independence of mind which was not lessened by the effects of leisure and flattery. The fantastic schemes of Marshal de MacMahon and some of his predecessors had given the Republic a few bad scares, and its leaders had decided to name no more marshals. Thus there remained within the gift of the Ministry of War one almost unattainable honor, a bait which unconsciously kept in line the more obstreperous spirits and left the realization of one great dream within the bounds of possibility.

However, the public demand for the sidetracking of Joffre forced the government to reconsider its decision. Almost the least solace that could be afforded the victor of the Marne was the presentation of a Marshal's baton. And the tranquil personality of Papa Joffre, his fifty years of faithful service, encouraged the government to feel that in this instance at least its generosity would meet with no ill reward. And at this time the decision was quite definite that only Joffre should be so honored.

But a year later, in 1918, an unexpected difficulty arose. The English generalissimo, Marshal Haig, was under the command of General Foch. And, although personal relations between the two men were excellent, it was deemed embarrassing for a Marshal to be subordinated to a mere general. British representations on this score forced the hand of Clemenceau, and so a second Marshal of France was named. But this seemed to the government a most dangerous elevation of a younger, altogether more fiery general, and so in order to counterbalance the personal prestige of the distinction it was decided that a plurality of Marshals was better than two in lonely grandeur. Therefore the victory celebrations saw the creation of a flock of new Marshals: Pétain, Fayolle, Franchet d'Esperey, Lyautey and even as posthumous honors, Gallieni and Maunoury.

But the elevation of Pétain with this second grouping gave little satisfaction to this pessimistic nature in which ambition had flowered so late and so vigorously. The elevation of Foch to the Interallied Command over the head of the commander-in-chief of French armies had been a bitter blow and the naming of Foch as Marshal, months before the second appointments, took most of the savor from the honor. Now the competition of the two men had assumed, for Pétain, an angrily personal aspect. Wherever he looked Foch was the victor, he himself only the second choice, the runner-up, the man passed over. Barely had the chances of war placed this long-time rival under his command than, by the interference of the British, the situation was reversed again. No, there was not much joy in being a run-of-the-mill Marshal when Foch once more possessed the senior title. Now, for the rest of their lives, Foch would be *the* Marshal, *the* conqueror. He, Pétain, was merely the conqueror of Verdun, one of a company with the colonial soldiers of yesteryear.

Furthermore there was nothing in the story of the war and its campaigns which seemed to Pétain to justify this reversal of due honors. During the early campaigns it had been Foch, the apostle of offense, who had been discredited by events and Pétain, the lifelong exponent of defense, who had shown what it could accomplish. Charleroi, Morhange, the whole course of the campaigns up until 1918, were vindications of Pétain in his own eyes, indictments of the theories of Foch. Where, then, was the justification for his honors? Victory, in the eyes of the new and unhappy Marshal, had come about not because of any superiority in the Foch tactics but because Ludendorff himself had fallen a victim of the snares of "Fochism," had attacked too violently and had exhausted himself too completely for any speedy recuperation.

Of course Foch's theory could not tally with this. The defensive tactics of the early months, he explained, had enabled the French to recoup their losses, to revise and build up their munitions supplies, and to mark time until the arrival of British and American reinforcements made possible the grand push. Beyond that they had no value since their major use had been the prolongation of the war and a sufficiency of men and supplies had made possible the *coup de grâce* by which alone the slaughter could be ended.

The prestige of Marshal Foch, and the undeniable results of his having been given authority and control at last, made his the prevailing viewpoint and, until the death of his rival, Marshal Pétain consumed in silence his disappointment and his sense of never having been given the opportunity of proving his point.

One significant result of the Foch-Pétain feud was its effect upon Pétain's theories of mechanized warfare. In November 1918 the Allies had more than seven hundred tanks in battle. Taken completely by surprise by this new weapon, the Germans had constructed only twenty-five of them, and the crushing weight of the tanks on the Allied side undoubtedly was one of the major factors which in the end broke the balance of power between the contending forces. The German General Staff never forgot this lesson. But Marshal Pétain never forgave the tanks. He has persisted to this day in regarding them as a freak weapon, one of the eccentricities of Foch and the British, and as possessed of no real or lasting influence upon the ancient science of war. And this is the major reason why French officers who have established tactical theories upon the force of armored units have found an obstinate and vindictive opponent in Marshal Pétain.

But, returning to the year of the Armistice and of pro-

motion, we find the new Marshals settling down to a peace
which all French people were desperately hoping would this
time be permanent. The army which had proved itself at such
cost on the battlefield was now popularly supposed to be
invincible, along with the generals who had guided it. And
now came another shift in the relationship between Foch and
Pétain. So long as the war lasted Foch was supreme as generalissimo of the Allied armies. But, with the signing of peace,
there no longer were any Allied armies. Foch was an idolized
leader without any tangible command. Pétain, however, remained in peacetime the generalissimo of all French forces,
so that his erstwhile superior no longer might exercise any
official superiority, although actually Foch's promotion had
predated that of Pétain. This was both illogical and unpleas-
ant but, sensing the tremendous popularity of Foch, Pétain
was sufficiently prudent to avoid all danger of an open clash.
He bided his time, nursed his grievances, took up again the
friendships broken by war and, incidentally, profited by the
impression of modesty to be gained from his silence.

And then, in 1924, Arabs of the Moroccan mountains of
the Riff began to revolt. Abd-el-Krim, chief of the rebellious
tribes, had succeeded in winning several attacks upon the
Spaniards. Then, taking refuge in the French protectorate,
he extended the scope of his raids and finally took to attacking the isolated French outposts.

An ambitious and daring chieftain, he entertained a dream
of conquering all of Morocco and of winning for himself an
African empire from which all Roumis would forthwith be
thrown into the sea. And fortune was with him at the start.
The French Republic was very tired of war and had returned
with determination to the old policy of thrift where military
expenditures were concerned. Furthermore she followed the

British policy of maintaining in her colonial outposts only the irreducible minimum of military forces. The small revolt soon took on the characteristics of a holy crusade and the task facing the small French force was crushing. The resident general, Marshal Lyautey, sent an urgent plea for reinforcements, but they were denied. Officials at home were in no mind to attach undue importance to the outbreak. French currency was slipping upon all the international markets and economy seemed the major need of the moment. However, under the insistence of Marshal Lyautey and the definite gains of the Arabs, France had to make up her mind whether she was prepared to evacuate Morocco and to abandon all that had been spent in developing that magnificent country, or whether she would immediately exert herself to re-establish order there.

Marshal Lyautey, first the conqueror and then the pacifier of Morocco, considered it somewhat as his personal domain. He begged for reinforcements and instead received good advice. He grew angry and importunate and so the politicians decided that he must be disciplined. They would entrust the saving of Morocco to a real soldier.

Now, throughout the Great War, Marshal Lyautey had remained by request at the head of his Moroccan protectorate. He had maintained there a state of complete and unquestioned loyalty to France. Not only had it been unnecessary for any French troops to police Morocco, but entire divisions of Moroccans had been recruited through his efforts to aid in the defeat of Germany. But it was true, nevertheless, that Lyautey's promotion to the rank of Marshal had not been won in combat with the Boches. Already a certain condescension was noticeable in the attitude of his fellow officers, who occasionally would refer to him as "Marshal for the Savage Tribes."

And so, since he had been unsuccessful in putting down

the revolt with the skeleton forces at his command, the occasion seemed propitious for his humiliation. It was decided that one of the heroes of 1918 should be asked to go to his assistance. Foch absolutely declined the assignment, not alone because he resented the slight to Marshal Lyautey but also because if he accepted he would be placing himself once more under the direction of his subordinate-superior, Marshal Pétain. And so the task fell at last upon the latter. It cannot have been unwelcome, for Marshal Lyautey, during his brief and stormy tenure as war minister, had been responsible for the appointment of Nivelle as commander-in-chief, in preference to Pétain. And the latter was not likely to have forgotten the fact. Now he was able to make his own conditions, which were that he should receive as many troops and as much matériel as he wished. Poor Lyautey had been refused fifty thousand troops but Marshal Pétain was granted, with alacrity, two hundred thousand men.

Lyautey, a wise and brave man, relinquished his army command and became merely the civil administrator of Morocco. And Marshal Pétain proceeded to organize his campaign. His first act was to establish contact with the Spanish Army and to arrange for operations to be conducted in common. His great personal prestige won for him concessions that the hidalgos never would have accorded to Lyautey, who had had to spend so much of his time in the past few years in the handling of petty border quarrels. And now to the Moroccans fell the honor of being slaughtered by a modern army, the same that had humbled the pride of the German Empire. The war of rifles and swords gave place to the war of howitzers, machine guns, flame throwers, planes, even tanks! Pétain could not afford to disdain the use of his nightmare weapon, secure as it was in the prestige of its war role. Modern matériel and the crushing weight of numbers ended the revolt within a few weeks, and Pétain returned to France with new glory. The increasing ranks of his admirers did not stop to reflect that if he had succeeded where Lyautey failed it was because the one could obtain no help and the other arrived armed with all the might of France. And the Moroccan campaign of Marshal Pétain against an ignorant and largely unarmed enemy was repeated a few years later in the tactics of the Italian invasion of Ethiopia.

Incidentally, it was during this campaign that the Marshal noted for future advancement two promising young officers, Colonel Corap and Lieutenant Colonel Giraud. Years later it was General Corap's army which suffered the initial shock of the German blitzkrieg in the break-through at Sedan. As to General Giraud, his remarkable adventures are too well known to require recapitulation here. But his extensive knowledge of the regions and tribes of North Africa is due to the fact that, following the Riff campaign, he remained in Africa until 1936, when he returned to France as a major general. The friendship of Marshal Pétain with the fateful clique of Spanish military politicos also was born at this time, when he first became acquainted with the dictator, Primo Rivera, General San Giurgio and the then insignificant Colonel Francisco Franco.

Pétain returned from Morocco on openly bad terms with Lyautey. To a newspaperman who congratulated the latter on his still-youthful appearance, the proconsul of Morocco replied: "I hope I don't have to die before Pétain. It would annoy me extremely to know that that fellow would orate at my funeral." Nevertheless Lyautey was not able to escape this irony. Upon his death at the age of eighty, Marshal Pétain, in full dress uniform, officiated as chief pallbearer.

The death of Marshal Foch in 1929 meant for Pétain at last complete supremacy in prestige and army control. But even this unmourned event brought to the waiting survivor a new embarrassment. The French Academy always invited to its membership the foremost men of the day, even when their pre-eminence had been gained in fields other than literature. Joffre, Poincaré, Clemenceau, Foch, had been received as the deaths of one after the other of the Forty Immortals left a vacant place. But Pétain's invitation came only when the death of Foch left vacant a place for him, and the tradition which makes it obligatory for the newly elected member to pronounce a panegyric upon his departed predecessor obliged Pétain to eulogize his ancient enemy for two long hours, before the remaining thirty-nine Immortals, who were perfectly conscious of the irony of the situation.

But at long last Pétain reigned alone. Joffre, who many years past had ceased to influence military thought, died in 1931. Fayolle had gone in 1928. Lyautey, heartsick and forgotten, was to die in hermitlike retirement upon his estate in Lorraine in 1934. Only Franchet d'Esperey still lived as a bedridden and almost senile invalid. Pétain alone remained as the survivor of all of the "Marshals of Victory."

Marshal Pétain was now the unquestioned authority on military matters for the succession of Ministers of War who followed each other on the Rue St. Dominique. And because of his supremacy as umpire, all the ambitious younger officers vied with each other to flatter him and humor his phobias. A word of approval from the Marshal could make a career. And, on the contrary, even the slightest expression of a differing opinion sufficed to disgrace those rash enough to voice it. The Marshal used this immense influence to develop, now unopposed, the full extent of his theories of defensive warfare. These he impressed on every possible occasion upon the minds of his obsequious young officer-companions and no good fortune attended those who occasionally voiced approval of the now despised theories of Foch. And the full flowering of these defensive theories was seen in the development of the System of Fortified Regions which became better, and more fatefully, known under the name of the Maginot Line.

Security for French frontiers, the education of army leaders to face all eventualities, protection of the country from possible invasion and a realistic evaluation of the new spirit already beginning to make itself felt across the Rhine: these were the responsibilities of Marshal Pétain, secure now in his pre-eminence. How did he acquit himself of them?

Clemenceau, who, as much as any man, was entitled to think of himself as France's savior, had been sidetracked, as soon as danger was averted, by the combined power of the horde of petty local politicians. The Tiger, watching from his distant retreat, often lashed himself into a fever of anxiety at their unawareness of danger, their preoccupation with the trivial. His prophetic judgment was delivered in his impassioned and brooding book, *The Grandeur and Misery of Victory*, which was published three years before Hitler began to loom as an evil shadow across the horizon of France.

"What a difference in mentality on the two sides of the Rhine," he proclaimed. "In Germany, every tightening of authority for the machine-drilling of men, with a view toward the most violent of offensives! With us, all the dislocations of slackness, and a fatuous reliance upon big words!"

Thus, even during the days of the Weimar Republic and in spite of the efforts of the mellifluous Stresemann, this great

Frenchman could see the storm clouds gathering. The Marshal, too, could see the same signs and portents which seemed so clear to Old Man Victory from his village in Vendée. But did he note the danger? Or was he more amenable to the spell of Aristide Briand, the assiduous apostle of an atmosphere of international laxity? Be that as it may, history records no such prescience on the part of the man who even at this early date had assumed complete moral responsibility for the defense of France against all comers.

Clemenceau also had his views upon the System of Fortified Regions:

"The fortified region system is to be applied solely to that part of the northeast frontier which stretches from Luxembourg to Switzerland. As regards the rest [the Franco-Swiss and Franco-Belgian frontiers], we rely upon Switzerland and Belgium to organize their German frontiers. Thus the great lesson of 1914 has been of no avail! . . . Various ministers have succeeded to the War Office since 1920. But there are, above them, military chiefs who have been the constant technical advisers of these men. *What have they done, these military chiefs, in the way of giving us a strong, unyielding frontier? Nothing! When have they made any protest against this lack of organization? Never!*"

Clemenceau, the civilian and patriot, had in 1930 warned the nation against the carelessness of its most responsible military leader. And, in view of the bounds with which the German menace grew within the next few years, how was the French army organized? Now solely under the control of Pétain, free from the influence of Foch, who had left it the most powerful and best organized army in Europe, it was completely a defensive army, unaggressive in spirit, insufficient in equipment and the knowledge of newer developments in war.*

Perhaps the most dangerous preoccupation of the petty bourgeois mind, which, after all, Pétain in essence possessed, was its yearning to conserve the small personal fortunes which, in spite of the tremors of inflation and the inroads of war, it had succeeded in amassing. All increases in the armaments budget tended to unbalance the stability of the currency, all new and heavier taxes, falling upon the wealthier classes, brought back again the specters of market crashes and inflation. The risk of war at this time seemed remote, but the risk of inflation was never very far distant.

It was of course preposterous not to see that it might become necessary for France to attack Germany either in self-defense or in fulfillment of one of her commitments to allies. France could not hope to crush Germany, with twice her population and five times her industrial power, without the help of powerful allies. These could come only from the east —from Russia, Poland, Rumania, Czechoslovakia. But the Marshal prepared only for one eventuality, the attack upon France by Germany, and he was not at all worried by that near-certainty, a German attack upon one of France's allies. His country was helpless when the need arose to rush to the assistance of Czechoslovakia, and thus came about the humiliation of Munich. And then again, when the French Army stood helplessly by to watch the crushing of the armies of its allies and friends, the Poles, it was the Marshal who had immobilized them within their barren fortifications. It was

* Notes appended to speeches in the Churchill collection, *While England Slept*, give the relative air strength of the leading powers in 1933 as: France, United States, Japan, Italy and Great Britain. A reference in the following year again places the French air power in the lead.

he who decreed that the army should have none of the equipment which would have enabled it to be of use to an embattled ally. This was illustrated again in 1940, when the need of turning to the aid of the Belgians and the Dutch brought the army pouring from the Maginot Line and precipitated the disaster of Sedan.

According to Clemenceau, the German Army, even five years before Hitler, was spending eight billions annually upon its army. But France in this year spent six billions. And even from this sum the Marshal was reapportioning the allotments for planes and tanks to the building of concrete fortifications.

The Marshal now had reached the stage which sometimes overtakes elderly and not too successful businessmen who have spent a lifetime at one aspect of their trade. His mind, never very elastic, had frozen into its narrow mold. He had no further interest in the theory of warfare outside his own conception of strategy. If he thought at all about the coming war, then gathering with the relentless and deliberate might of an avalanche, he thought of it as an opportunity to prove once and for all that defense would triumph—that Foch with his slashing theories of attack, attack, and still attack, had been a fool for luck whereas to Pétain would accrue the delayed admiration of a world at last realizing his inevitable rightness.

Actually he knew nothing and cared nothing for the tremendous differences which the advent of airplanes and mechanized vehicles had made to the ancient realities of war. Fascinated by the vistas opened to them by the use of tanks and all that they implied, the German generals had applied their keen minds and competitive spirit to devising campaigns built upon the new weapons. Furthermore they studied and improved upon these weapons, planned new uses for them and adapted them to the standardized techniques of battle. They invented nothing new and indeed they had no need for invention. The great ideas had been born upon our side during the war years. The Germans brought to them only the sharp attention of good minds undulled by complacency and indolence. Furthermore Marshal Pétain even made them a present of part of their thinking. For it was during these early thirties that the young Major Charles de Gaulle wrote *Vers Une Armée de Metier*, a book of which the German generals immediately saw the importance and the ingenuity but which was treated by Marshal Pétain with a studied disdain. Only when it was too late was it possible to see how greatly indebted to De Gaulle was the German genius, the bold conception of Paulus, Rommel, Guderian, Von Blomberg, Von Brauchitsch. And their studies were attended by no difficulties evolved in France. So elaborate was Marshal Pétain's disapproval of this boldness of plan on the part of a young unknown that he failed even to reserve its publication rights for the French Army. The officers of any army in the world could buy, study and export it.

And yet an army built upon *Le Système de Gaulle* would in 1939 have permitted France to rush to the rescue of Poland, to invade German territory and to force one half of the Hitlerian armies to face about and fight in the west. This modern army could have won in Belgium instead of being outclassed by the rush of German motorized divisions.

A mellower, more human commander than the Marshal might have reflected, when this ambitious small book by a young man brave enough to state his theories in face of a static concept of war frozen in the pattern of twenty years ago was placed before him, on the time when his young and, in their place, perfectly sound, theories of warfare, were being ignored for the showier concept of attack. But no such memories came to mind. Indeed the one book on warfare which received any notice from him was a publication issued in 1939 by one of his most assiduous admirers, General Chauvineau. Its title was, *Is an Invasion Still Possible?* And for two hundred and fifty pages it elaborately disproved both possibility and probability. Taking as his thesis the moral unlikelihood and the physical impossibility (in 1939!) of invasion, General Chauvineau went on to ask why France should fritter away her strength upon superfluous alliances, with their hint that at some time or other she might find herself militarily obligated to fight with Russia or Poland or Czechoslovakia, or even England? Such thinking was of course, in spite of its tragic blindness, in line with the wishful reasoning of the men who engineered and applauded the "realism" of Munich.

Chauvineau's book appeared in that waiting interlude between Munich and Sedan. In it he took occasion to rebuke the "childish and ridiculous affirmation" of Major de Gaulle that one hundred thousand professional soldiers equipped with completely modern matèriel would be sufficient to assure victory to their side. Only a few months were necessary to test the ridiculous affirmation, and by then a force which experts since have estimated never at any one moment exceeded two hundred and fifty thousand trained troops, had vanquished three million Poles, four hundred thousand Hollanders, one hundred thousand Belgians, five million Frenchmen and half a million Englishmen. These were the picked battle troops whose organization and training had been envisioned by De Gaulle. The masses of the German soldiery came into the picture later, for the occupation and "pacification" of the conquered lands.

But here are some quotations from the preface written for this ignorant and bumptious book by the man responsible for the military destinies of France—and written, never forget, in the fateful year of 1939!

"Consider the tank," said the Marshal, "regarded today as so incomparable an offensive instrument. How much greater would its efficiency be, used as a weapon of defense or even of counterattack against an enemy who, though armored, is disorganized by the very fact of his advance. . . . Transportation of equipment, men and supplies, by road or rail, is always more favorable to the defense than to the attacker. . . . The defense has become so powerful now that it is necessary for any attacker to possess enormous superiority; he must have three times the manpower, six times the artillery and twelve times the ammunition to be able even to hope to dominate the defense.

"What would become of an offensive of armored divisions," continued the Marshal's preface, "if it were forced to encounter divisions of the same type but already in position on a battlefield of their choice and curtained by anti-tank artillery fire, reinforced by mine fields and connected with natural obstacles?"

One might at least conclude from this that the Marshal, having considered the possibility that any invader of France would approach with these mechanized divisions, had taken full precautions by providing that the enemy would be met by these "divisions of the same type," protected by their natural and man-made obstacles. But in this same fateful year of 1939, France was able to oppose only two divisions of tanks to ten German divisions! And for this complete inadequacy, for the whole spirit of unpreparedness which permeated the army's supplies, Marshal Pétain must bear the major share of responsibility. Not only was he the nation's military head but for years preceding 1934 he had been generalissimo; in 1934 he was Minister of War, and after 1935 he was military adviser to the successive ministries. The Maginot Line was his brain child and his darling, and every American correspondent of that time is able to verify the excessive pride with which he discoursed upon its wonders.

And yet, tragic failure though it was, the vast concrete graveyard of France's hopes, one might have expected that a jealous care of its secrets would have been the Marshal's policy. But it was not so. Henri de Kerillis, a former friend of the Marshal and the one deputy of the Right who voted against the Munich Pact, has described in his book, *Français, Voici la Vérite*, how the tremendous task of electrifying the Maginot Line was handed over in its entirety to a subsidiary branch of the House of Siemens, most famous of all German engineering firms. All the blueprints of the fortified region were given into the hands of this entrenched Nazi corporation! For this the Marshal can find no excuses. The Maginot Line was his. He approved every detail, every contract for work. He could not have failed to know who was prying into the secrets of his defense.

CHAPTER 4

WHOM THE GODS WOULD DESTROY . . .

THERE HAD NEVER been much sympathy between Philippe Pétain and the bosses of the Third Republic's political machine. As a young man whose aristocratic pretensions were acquired, not inherited, he had, in order to impress his well-born and reactionary friends, affected an attitude *plus royaliste que le Roi*. Thus, in his cautious young soul, he sought to offset what to him was the disadvantage of plebeian birth. As the years passed an affectation of the attitude of mind he secretly admired came to be second nature. Instinctively he disliked the rough-and-tumble of democratic politics and it was not difficult for him to seek, and find, many reasons for distrust and dislike of the Republic and its elected officers.

With the endless weighing and balancing which went on in his secretive mind, all of the missed chances of his life began to seem solely the fault and responsibility of the Republic. The fact that, had it not been for the war, he would have been placed upon the retirement list as a mere colonel became the fault of the Republic. The promotion of Nivelle before himself, the acceptance by France of England's insulting demand that Foch, not he, should be the interallied generalissimo—all this was the fault of the Republic, influenced by the English. The ingratitude of the government became a quiet obsession, difficult to understand except by a con-

sideration of the rigid mind and the overweening ambition
of this determinedly discontented man. All his honors were
Dead Sea fruit because they came too late, because a rival had
preceded him, because they were grudgingly given.

It must be admitted, however, that following the Dreyfus
affair and the segregation of Church and State, the ascendancy
of the republican parties brought inevitable abuses and these
in their turn, as is the cycle with American political parties,
gradually and inevitably rebuilt the strength of the opposition.

Before 1908 the Royalist or reactionary party was mainly
represented by a handful of noisy young men with little
practical influence and not even a modicum of the tact which
attracts the voters to the bandwagon. But the party in power
degenerated progressively. The great Republicans who had
fought for Dreyfus and who saw the ideals of the Third Republic as living realities were succeeded by hard-headed machine politicians closely allied with profiteers. Their organization no longer sent to Parliament men capable of winning
respect for the Republic or willing to subordinate themselves
to the national good. On the contrary the type of man elected
in increasing numbers to both houses was the shrewd and
calculating individual, fully aware of the vote-getting value
of small concessions, willing to trade a road here, a bridge
there, a job somewhere else, in exchange for a bloc of votes.

Furthermore the new generation of Republicans was one
willing to take full advantage of that flaw in the Republic's
laws which enabled an elected representative to continue to
prosecute his private business, unless and until he became a
cabinet minister. This encouraged a flock of astute lawyer-
politicians to run for office. One of the most brazen of these
was Alexandre Millerand, who was head of his party when it
succeeded in passing the laws against ecclesiastical tax exemp-

tions. This did not prevent him from defending many an important clerical client and from collecting in fees more than a million francs. Nor did he suffer politically from the well-known amount of his enrichment, for just fifteen years later he became president of the Republic without any open expression of disapproval from the French people.

Each new election saw the ranks of the clever and greedy young men among the government's supporters strengthened and thereby rendered more cynical. Idealism became ridiculous and a devotion to the Republic meant either an unbearably old-fashioned innocent re-elected in spite of the machine's best efforts by unbearably old-fashioned rural constituents or else it constituted one of the purely perfunctory phrases of campaign oratory, tacitly admitted by everybody to sound pretty and mean nothing.

The entrenched corruption of this group had reached its full strength when the first World War broke out. Upon the incorruptible few still remaining—Poincaré, Barthou, Clemenceau—fell the heroic task of cleaning house and at the same time prosecuting a disastrous war. Clemenceau proved himself in this period worthy of Danton and Robespierre. He arrested and brought to trial the then Minister of the Interior, Louis Malvy, a horrible example of the local machine boss at his worst. Malvy had a long record as a manipulator of majorities and he had, in the midst of war, subsidized with state money a whole group of newspapers, the editors of which were working for Germany. Malvy was sentenced, but in 1925 he won a pardon and, hitching his star to that of Pierre Laval, he succeeded in becoming once more a figure of political importance.

Joseph Caillaux, leader of the Conservative Center in the Senate, also was arrested by Clemenceau and was tried and condemned for secret dealings with the enemy. Caillaux was negotiating with Germany for a surprise peace, declaration of which was to hinge upon his being called to power by the next parliamentary crisis. He was as assured of France's military defeat at that time as, twenty-one years later, we find Pétain to be, and his reaction was the same.

In his memoirs Clemenceau makes a comment upon Caillaux which he might well have made regarding Pétain in the dark days of 1940. He said: "When I tried to explain M. Caillaux to myself, I just supposed that he regarded the country as done for, and that he was anticipating every means of currying favor with Germany."

Clemenceau also had to arrest Senator Charles Humbert, a henchman of the great steel cartel, the Comité des Forges, who while maintaining a front of devout patriotism was actively campaigning for consistent overproduction and at the same time was obtaining for sale to Germany the secret figures on French armaments reserves. Four men were shot in this drastic housecleaning, Bolo Pasha, Lenoir and Desouches, for having conspired to sell the newspaper Le Journal to the Germans, and a deputy named Turmel, who sold confidential parliamentary information to the enemy. It was thanks to Clemenceau that these Augean stables were cleaned and that good Frenchmen were able to lead the country to victory.

But, once the danger was ended, the incorrigible professional politicians crawled out once more from their hiding places. Clemenceau, the wartime savior, was a victim of that ingratitude which forgetful democrats too often accord to their best friends. Removed from power, Clemenceau lived in obscurity, writing furiously his unheeded and well-merited warnings. Pierre Laval, the obsequious little peasant politician, was busily sowing the seeds of his future dominance in the middle twenties. He recalled from obscurity the erstwhile traitors Malvy and Caillaux, and vague stories of treason were forgotten by the shortsighted constituents in favor of the immediate bribe of a new railroad terminus, the building of an armory, the enlargement of a military garrison with its consequent largesse to the businessmen of a small community. In no time at all both men were reinstated in public confidence, appointed, Malvy for the Chamber of Deputies, Caillaux for the Senate, to the important posts of chairmen of the Finance commissions. Both of them were among the assiduous supporters of Laval at the time of the Armistice.

Clemenceau died, abandoned and half forgotten. But before the end he penned some further prophecies for the heedless nation.

"We are constantly hearing about the superman. And the subman; what of him? . . . Nations now living are coming to an end. Our consciousness of our own freedom to act entails the fixing of responsibility. France will be what the men of France deserve."

Once again scandals began to accumulate. Republican constituents began to realize, belatedly, the harm being done to the very fabric of the Republic by the growing disrepute of parliamentary representatives.

The President of the Republic, Deschanel, the man who had been preferred to Clemenceau once the war was won, was found one morning wandering along the railroad tracks in his pajamas. Completely insane, he had jumped from the window of his private train. His days were ended in a padded cell, a circumstance which, while reflecting no discredit upon him, did not tend to restore confidence in the sorely beset Third Republic. A former finance minister, Lucien Klotz, was arrested for the distinctly plebeian vice of passing worthless checks. Raoul Peret, speaker of the Chamber of Deputies, was gravely compromised by the crash of the Oustric Bank, which involved a four-hundred-million-franc swindle.

Public opinion looked upon these manifestations with growing concern. Earlier republics had fallen. Was it possible that this one too was in danger? And now the voice of the reactionary was loud in the land.

Italy was the new model. Since 1922, by the simple process of suppressing all opposition, Mussolini had outlawed public scandal in Rome. This, for simple souls, proved that fascism had thereby eradicated scandal. The Rightist press of France knew well how to exploit this notion.

And then, in 1933, a world-shaking manifestation was vouchsafed the world, which regarded it for the most part with blank incomprehension. Hitler became first chancellor, then Fuehrer, of the German Reich. One of his first acts was to provide Germany with a Minister of Propaganda.

The French, who have a lively sense of the ridiculous, found this thoroughly entertaining. They wrote comic songs and sang them with gusto, and caricatured, in print and on the stage, the antics of the ludicrous little Dr. Goebbels. But the activities in France of Dr. Goebbels were not at all laughable. German money now began to subsidize a whole new branch of the venal press, and the existing Rightist newspapers began a subtle new line of antidemocratic propaganda. Le Jour, Candide, Gringoire were all too clever to attack the Republic openly, but one after another leading Republicans were lampooned with brilliant and merciless ridicule. Unhappily there was always a real scandal of one sort or another to lend verisimilitude to imaginary or exaggerated misbehavior on the part of parliamentarians. French law offers little defense against printed political calumny and the public began to echo the censorious tone of the newspapers.

As soon as the lavish supply of German money had been sufficiently advertised, new and grasping little men began affiliating themselves with the anti-Republican, antidemocratic, anti-Semitic campaigns. France was not at war with Germany and there was nothing to prevent business relationships on both sides of the border. Many French writers and publicists were notoriously careless in marking a line between the legitimate interchange of literary merchandise and the acceptance of pay for the deliberate dissemination at home of foreign and dangerous doctrines. Furthermore it began to be increasingly difficult, among the clashes of personalities and ambitions, for the disinterested to see clearly just where the interest of the country lay. A breach too wide for bridging was growing between the Left and the Right.

In all of this the tragedy of a press that could be bought and sold played an increasingly ominous part. "Patriotic" newspapers contented themselves with accepting the pay of the government. But the number of these was dwindling while the flock which quite happily accepted or even begged for German or Italian money was growing weekly. Less important papers received funds from smaller, less menacing neighbors.

These transactions usually were negotiated in Switzerland, sometimes quite openly. Otto Abetz, the German wholesaler in French literary consciences, was charming and sympathetic, and always available. He had millions in cash for disposal and unlimited supplies of not always subtle flattery. Young and practically unknown writers, starving for success, received magnificent contracts for the translation of their work into German. Others, whose books seemed obviously unlikely to interest German readers, were employed to translate into French the work of rising young Nazi authors. This work was lavishly rewarded, and in addition the dazzled employees were invited to visit Germany, where they met with the flattering receptions accorded to great men. Within a few years a literary nucleus, thoroughly sold on the Nazi idea, was dwelling in France with German support.

Remembering the completeness with which Charles A. Lindbergh was seduced into an awestruck admiration of the might of the German Reich, it is not hard to see how these small fry, for whom recognition at home had been hard to win and slow in coming, were won by such treatment. Once the German frontier was crossed, the lavish rewards of true merit were at hand! The compliments of the Fuehrer himself, the magnificent receptions of Goering and Goebbels—these, and the cash rewards—completely won such men as Jean Luchaire; the fulsome and tireless admirer of Fascist strength, Alphonse de Chateaubriant; Benoist-Mechin; Drieu-La-Rochelle; Louis Ferdinand Céline. These spoke and wrote on all possible occasions of the splendor of the Reich and the desirability of a true appreciation of the Nazi leaders.

The Third Republic was now gravely ill. Drastic and selfless surgery still might have saved her, but the surgeon was not there. Her case took a new turn for the worse with the advent of the Stavisky scandals in 1933-34, and the end was the sorry agony of 1940 when a brave and gallant history was terminated, "not with a bang, but a whimper," by callous and ambition-ridden men. These six years marked a progressive decadence in France's conduct toward herself; in the political conscience of the electors, who no longer thought of their responsibility for the type of man now making a mockery of republican government; in the behavior of these men themselves, who had reduced to a formula the mechanics of purchasing voters with small and concrete favors while selling the vital interests of the people and their country to the highest bidder. During these years was born the superficial and unthinking comparison of the laxity of democracies with the cast-iron order of the authoritarian regimes. Forgotten was the truth that a democracy must earn by unceasing watchfulness its political health and harmony. Unheeded was the warning: "France will be what the men of France deserve."

Stavisky was a fantastic villain even for France, which liked her swindlers to be picturesque. Summarized, he was a common adventurer of Russian extraction, many times condemned for larceny and swindling, who had so built up his political connections that he was able, upon being arrested for still another felony, to remain out on bail for years on end. His powerful friends managed to defer his court appearances for season after season. In the meantime he labored industriously to increase the sum of his depredations to a total still unmatched—five hundred million francs!

He passed as a financier, honest and charming as he was wealthy. With his beautiful wife he received the elite of Paris. Ministers, deputies, senators, owners of theaters and newspapers—all were proud to be on the visiting list of "M. Alexandre."

Hitler and his wholesale seizures have since made such adventures as that of "M. Alexandre" seem fairly picayune. For this small-time robber seized control only of one small city, that of Bayonne. Nevertheless his methods were interesting. All the civil servants of any importance in the town were members of the Stavisky gang. And pretty soon the issue of bonds of the city of Bayonne mounted into astronomical numbers. The bonds of course carried the guarantee of the French government and competition for them was keen. All that were thrown on the market were snatched by banks who thus invested the funds of their depositors. The sale was further aided by the personal endorsement of several ministers, who called the attention of bank presidents to these "interesting" issues.

This soaring scaffolding finally collapsed on the inevitable day when the city of Bayonne (30,000 population) no longer could honor the coupons on these huge loans. Newspapers began to take an interest in Bayonne, a score of banks became alarmed and then angry, and the game was up. The swindle totaled around half a billion francs, and the successful swindler was a former jailbird, a man who even now was stalling off prosecution thanks only to the agility of his lawyers and the extent to which he had corrupted a variety of important politicians.

Stavisky fled. Police tracked him to a mountain cabin near the Swiss-Alpine border. The mystery of his fate has never received an entirely adequate explanation, for he was found dead of a bullet in his head. The government, with scarcely concealed relief, described it as the suicide of a desperate fugitive. The opposition made no bones about calling it murder, undertaken to silence permanently what looked like being an appalling string of confessions and implications.

For months the French newspapers spoke of nothing else, and the scandalmongers had a field day. Among the older, watchfully waiting, more cautious anti-Republicans, the rejoicing was scarcely less open. Here at last was the opportunity to "strangle the Slut."

In many respects the Chautemps government occupied an

indefensible position. It could not deny that nineteen deferments of Stavisky's trial had been obtained solely through the power and influence of his lawyers, and that these lawyers, in turn, were among the strongest supports of the Republican majority. Since French judges are appointed, not elected, and since these men exercised a powerful control over appointments, no judicial voice was raised in protest against the unseemly proceeding.

And the name of Premier Camille Chautemps was openly mentioned among those of the powerful protectors of Stavisky. Chautemps, many times prime minister, was chairman of the Radical Party, and several times Minister of Justice. Undoubtedly there were judges of sufficient character to condemn a defendant whose advocate was a past, and possibly a future, Minister of Justice. But the decision would have been a hard one. It was much simpler, and equally satisfactory to everybody concerned, simply to delay the trial until the next session in order to accommodate President Chautemps and his friend President Dalimier, both very busy men.

Neither could the government deny that not only many important political figures but also high police officials were perfectly well acquainted with the checkered past of Alexandre Stavisky. These last also remained silent out of a wish not to embarrass the swindler's powerful protectors. Stavisky was at this time rumored to be one of the largest contributors to the campaign fund of the Radical Party and to have paved the way for its triumph in 1932 with large chunks of his dubiously acquired wealth.

But the most compromised public figure of all was the prosecuting attorney for the Republic, Justice Pressard, who happened, perhaps by coincidence, to be a brother-in-law of Chautemps. He committed suicide and shortly after one of his assistants, a Counselor Prince, who had imprudently announced his intention of revealing important secrets, was found dead and horribly crushed upon the railroad tracks. There was a clamor of "suicide" by friends of the government and countercharges of assassination by its critics. The nation was outraged. At no time was dissatisfaction with the men who now were mishandling the Republic at greater heat.

It was still possible for the Republicans to mend their waning prestige. A stern, impartial inquiry, conducted by representatives of all parties, and an absolute determination to reveal the truth and deal justice wherever the chips might fall, could have accomplished much in reassuring the people. But Chautemps decided otherwise. An inquest was decided upon and the jury was stacked carefully with his own henchmen. A judgment whitewashing everybody concerned with the exception of a pathetic scapegoat, a minor police officer named Bonny, was returned and public unrest grew stronger.

The injudiciousness of permitting a man under suspicion to dominate an inquiry into so grave a scandal, the obstinacy of that man and his shortsighted conviction that he could still control the dangerous situation, were the rocks upon which the Radical Party wrecked itself and in doing so dealt further shattering blows at the tottering prestige of parliamentary government in France. This same Chautemps, it should be remembered, is the man who paved the way in 1940 for the Pétain coup d'état. For years before this sorry climax he had been working wholeheartedly toward the corruption of his nation from within. His is one of the major responsibilities for the long downward trail and the eventual debacle.

From now on the Radical Party, which had represented the great majority of moderate Republicans, was deprived of the very elements which had given it stability and power. The active and intelligent middle-class minds who had been its chief support now deserted in disgust. And they realigned themselves according to their sympathies with German, Italian or Russian-inspired groups.

As one example, membership of the fascist Croix de Feu increased within a few days from thirty thousand to 1,200,000 and other similar organizations showed corresponding membership increases. At the same time adherents of the Confédération Générale du Travail, the main trades union confederation, grew in 1936 from less than a million members to a total of 5,300,000. And the Communist and Socialist parties were able to show a correspondingly impressive increase.

The Radical Party, thus reduced, rallied around its honest stalwart, Edouard Herriot, and his disciple Daladier. These two men still might have saved it, but it had neither the courage nor the ruthlessness to purge itself of the Chautemps clique. It never was able to recover its former standing.

A country so torn among extremist factions and unable to confide its government to one dominant party is launched upon the road to civil war. And where military sympathy can be enlisted in the name of restoring order, the danger becomes a real one. So far, in spite of their recent accretions, the parties of the Right had been unable to select a leader around whom possible revolutionaries might group themselves. Far too conspicuous in their counsels were such vacuous individuals as Leon Daudet, pedants such as Maurras or sheer windbags of the type of Louis Marin. These were not material out of which stirring leadership might be fashioned.

And so it was that in January 1934 the restless and now hopeful enemies of the Third Republic turned their attention to Marshal Pétain. He, the venerable and austere hero of a

population sick of politicians, would provide an admirable
front for a consolidation of Rightist forces. Moreover, there
was reason to believe that the suggestion would not be unwelcome. But the old man felt that prudence was indicated. He
assured the petitioners of his sympathy, promised his influence
with the army, but begged to remain anonymous for the
time being.

On February 6, 1934, the revolt broke out. Uttering cries
of "Long live Pétain! We want Pétain!" the fascist mob
rushed across the Champs Elysées and attempted to force the
Alexandre III Bridge so as to seize the Chamber of Deputies
and thus overthrow the Republic. Daladier, then prime minister, gave the order to the troops to open fire, as it was his
right and his duty to do. He resigned immediately, convinced
that his career was now ruined forever. Twenty men were
killed, a thousand wounded. Thus the German Ministry of
Propaganda, plus French political blundering, had in little
more than a year transformed civilized, self-possessed France
into a witches' cauldron where all of the evil and disparate
elements of civil war were fusing themselves into a terrible
whole.

In a desperate effort to appease the factionalists and to
restore some semblance of national unity, President Albert
Lebrun organized a Government of Union, representing all
parties but the Socialists and Communists. His aim was to
place in the public eye as many new or at least innocuous
persons as possible. Herriot left the chairmanship of the
Chamber which had kept him out of the turmoil and took
his place in the new cabinet, which also included Laval and
Flandin.

And now a new disappointment awaited the watching
Marshal. The well-instructed crowds who had been repulsed

in their abortive attempt to snatch power had dutifully called upon the Marshal. Although their movement had been ill managed and ill advised, as the Marshal had shrewdly suspected it might be, nevertheless the fact that a large group of discontented people dashed into battle shouting his name should, he felt, have had some weight once the revolt was overthrown. He had, indeed, felt himself sure of new honors whichever side won out. The revolutionaries would promptly have enthroned him as their figurehead had they won, and the astonishing evidence of his popularity should reasonably have persuaded the conciliatory and frightened President to choose him as the unifying figure.

Alas, the President had no such thought. For a prime minister he turned to the amiable, honest and thoroughly Republican Gaston Doumergue, a former President, who passed his time when out of office trimming rosebushes in the country in perfect and unambitious good humor. And the Marshal must, perforce, nurse in silence his anger and disappointment. He was, it is true, named Minister of War in the Doumergue Cabinet, but this was a small sop to a man who had hoped himself to name the Minister of War.

But from this moment on the French Army was solely in the hands of one man. To his complete military power was added the civilian administrative function. And if the French people considered this circumstance at all, it was with satisfaction that, come what may, the destinies of their army were entrusted to the hero of Verdun.

Maxime Weygand had followed Pétain as generalissimo but he was not the type of man who would dare, whatever the provocation, to oppose his hierarchical chief. Pétain had upon his sleeve one more star than Weygand and, for the latter, this sufficed. The habits of obedience, of a total discipline acquired in more than fifty years of a military career, can create almost physical reflexes. It is a psychological form of learning to swim. No man who has once learned can abandon himself to drowning, and no man who has subjected himself wholly to a narrow and caste-ridden military system for the greater part of his life can suddenly begin questioning the orders of a superior. When Pétain spoke, Weygand jumped. Even following the armistice in North Africa, when every dictate of reason urged him to disapprove of Pétain's decision, General Weygand still could not bring himself to open disobedience. And during the shoddy drama of Vichy, it was never the generals or the admirals grown gray in service who found the courage to disobey or to resist, when a Marshal of France spoke. The exceptions which confirm the rule are interesting. General de Gaulle, youngest general in the army, had not yet been broken in to these reflexes. Furthermore he was an obstinate young man with strong convictions who had chosen to become a Jeremiah, warning an unheeding France of the dangers ahead. General Catroux, who for years had been a wise and progressive governor-general of Indo-China, had learned during his long exiles to meet situations requiring quick thought by making his own decisions.

But now the Marshal was to know the joys of absolute power over the army. Or so it may briefly have seemed. Actually, however, the absolute power of any bureaucrat is limited by the supervision and control of the legislative branch of government. This, of course, is the protection of the citizens of democracies but it is an endless and intolerable affront to possessors of the naturally autocratic spirit. And the Marshal's is such a spirit, nurtured and made strong by the inevitable authoritarianism of army life, plus the constant companionship of reactionaries. The endless adulation of subordinates, bankers, industrialists, aristocrats and prelates was soon to give way to the everlasting sniping of the petty parliamentarians. These small lawyers and rural politicians had no false respect for the white hairs of France's sole surviving marshal. Their criticism was constant, disrespectful, often ill informed and spiced with coarse sarcasm. But occasionally, which was even worse, it was surprisingly pungent and pertinent. The Marshal, to whom the habit of command now was second nature, had to listen, to seem meek, even to reply to these disgusting creatures. Inch by inch he debated his decisions with these big frogs from small puddles who were entitled thus to hound him only by virtue of the ridiculous system which elected them members of the committee on finances or military affairs. How easy it would have been for the righteous and the competent to govern France for her own good had these absurd and pretentious chatterers, these "six hundred little kings of France" been returned firmly to the oblivion they deserved!

The Marshal differed from Hitler at this point only in the fact that his revolt against the "tyranny" of parliamentary government had grown more slowly, had taken root in a colder, more cautious and self-distrustful nature, and had never known the fanatic fire which consumed Hitler. Circumstance was to make of the Marshal merely a pale and plotting copy of the master tyrant, never an equal or even a respected second. But his state of mind at this point resembled that of Hitler in 1932 when he described the existence of an army within a democracy as contradictory and mutually destructive.

With this theory, and Hitler's expression of its undesirability, the Marshal must wholeheartedly have agreed at this time. All his glory, all his authority, were insufficient to close the mouth of a wretched little Socialist lawyer who might even be a Jew into the bargain. For the Marshal was in close agreement also with Hitler on the question of Jews. The Jew also was obstinate and prone to argue with authority in the person of the Marshal. Hitler had said that during all of his long propaganda campaigns he had never succeeded in convincing a Jew, "and that is why I hate that people." *

It was during this period of his life that the Marshal began to find the experiences of the two dictators "very interesting." Some such robust power as theirs was necessary if France was to be saved from herself. Pétain at this time was still a patriotic Frenchman. He did not realize the extent to which the suborned Rightist press which had made of him a figurehead was using him for destructive ends. But these newspapers kept up an endless stream of contempt and belittlement for the democracies, of praise and envy for the new, strong, rejuvenated Axis nations. Why could not France too be born anew, was their cry. And it was one which found a ready listener in the discontented old man, coming too late to a first-hand battle of wits with the agents of democratic government and utterly unequipped by temperament or training to regard his experience with tolerance or humor.

It was necessary of course, before any great headway could be made with this campaign, to wean France from her stubborn attachment for England. In spite of a mistrust born of misunderstanding, and an almost permanent exasperation, the British-French alliance had endured well. It had been, perhaps, a marriage of convenience in the beginning. But it had lasted with the strength such marriages sometimes develop, and a bond of somewhat cynical affection was firmly established between the two. It had been a real grief to the

* *Mein Kampf.*

French, as the most sentimental of the partners, when the British entered their critical phase in the years soon after the Armistice. The British, removed from the chronic terrors of the Rhine border, were not far from superciliousness in their comments upon the nervousness of the French. They, who also took the alliance so much for granted that they did not feel it necessary to be overly polite about it, would probably have been shocked and appalled had they realized to what extent their complacent shortsightedness was aiding the enemies of France within and without that sorely beset land.

Pétain, as we have seen, had never particularly loved the English. And now the Rightist papers which were so flattering in their references to him broke out in a rash of inspired anti-British articles and forecasts with most of which the Marshal found himself in secret agreement. Henri Béraud, a typical example of the formerly impoverished Leftist who found prosperity with a change of conviction, set the pattern for most of these with his provocative and insulting: "Must England Be Reduced to Slavery?" M. Béraud, translated from nonentity to fame of a sort, took to sporting a monocle in his calls at the boudoirs of the "noble Faubourg," whence so much of his mischief-making inspiration emanated in these days of Dr. Goebbels' most assiduous ground-breaking.

The Marshal now was emerging from the intellectual shell under which he had hidden for so long. The greater part of his life had been passed in the somewhat stereotyped atmosphere of military college. Then, after a brief burst of glory, he had retired again into a disciplined aura from which his pronouncements issued with something of the awesome effect of holy writ. This new experience of political officeholding came with devastating effect into a life now set in molds of cast-iron rigidity. Controversy which he regarded as insolent attended his actions, ignoramuses to whom Verdun was but a name dared to argue his decisions, his logic. He envied the men who with vigor and daring had rid themselves of such bumptious interference. He now began to think how fittingly his long career would be crowned with a deathless glory could he rid France of this democratic germ which paralyzed and corrupted the life of a once great country.

Ideas took root slowly in the Marshal's mind, but once there they remained to stay. Between 1934 and 1940 this thought returned many times, took shape and finally crystal-lized into an old man's obsession. He had always been some-what susceptible to flattery. Now, as age dimmed the normal critical faculties, it became a necessity of life. No proposal seemed to register unless it was surrounded with flowery encomiums. And naturally the men whose business it was to size up and make use of the weaknesses of their fellows took full advantage of this one. It was fatally easy to hold out the bait of one day becoming France's "Social Messiah," as a fitting climax to the career of her military savior. And one of the horrors of Vichy has been that the obstinacy of a life-time plus the clouded vision of old age combined to convince France's betrayer that he is, in truth, her savior!

His followers now claimed that in him lay vested the only hope of ever bringing order out of the chaos that France now was. Letters addressed to him began more and more to fol-low the formula, as they still do, of: "You, yourself, M. le maréchal, you alone who know better than anybody else . . ." and so forth. It is small wonder that to his own unshaken belief in his rightness there came to be added a conviction of predestination, of omnipotence and omniscience. Almost without his being aware of it he became the acknowledged figurehead behind whom gathered the dissatisfied, the schemers, the industrialists who disliked the new demands of the working classes, the wealthy idlers who disapproved of the new taxes.

Upon this situation, the assassination in Marseilles of King Alexander of Yugoslavia and Louis Barthou, Minister of Foreign Affairs and almost the last of the truly great statesmen of the Third Republic, fell with crushing force. Mussolini had instigated the murder, and had thus at one blow deprived France of her best minister, one of her surest allies and friends and a large share of what remained of her crumbling faith in the servants of the Republic. The French people were horror-stricken as details began to reveal the inertia, the sheer stupidity, of Albert Sarraut, Minister of the Interior, who was charged with the safety of France's royal guest and who had done absolutely nothing to protect him. Actually he had been notified by agents of the Deuxième Bureau that two well-known political assassins had crossed the Franco-Italian border. No steps had been taken to check on their whereabouts or to keep them forcibly out of mischief during the visit. Naturally, the Rightist press did not forbear to point out that such criminal stupidity never occurred in the fascist countries.

Sarraut was a well-meaning but quite incapable nonentity, co-owner of one of the largest and most influential provincial newspapers, La Dépêche de Toulouse. This paper exercised a strong influence over the elections in fourteen out of the eighty-eight French departments, so that eighty deputies out of six hundred owed their jobs to the good will of the Sarraut brothers. Maurice, who was actual publisher, was a strong influence behind the Radical throne, since he could with a gesture control the disposition of eighty votes. It was these eighty votes which won for Albert Sarraut, who had no other qualification, a post of some sort or other in practically every Radical cabinet. Following the assassination, public grief and rage forced him into temporary retirement, but he was soon back in power again. It was the seeming impossibility of ridding politics of this type of hanger-on that was beginning to discourage even the sanguine and sensible men among France's democrats.

A few days later Herriot resigned, causing the fall of the Doumergue Cabinet, and the Marshal was free to return to privacy. Paradoxically, although he had hated his public life, he was annoyed at the manner of its ending. Technically, since he was forced out, he had slipped down a rung in the climb to power. His unforgiving mind fastened upon Edouard Herriot as the author of this setback and it is characteristic that one of his first acts upon assuming complete control of France was the revocation of Herriot's mayoralty of Lyons, an office that the great-hearted democrat had held for almost thirty-six years, to the satisfaction of everybody concerned. Herriot, after the defiant and ringing warning: "It is impossible that liberty should die in the country of its birth"—a warning which the Marshal must have found exceptionally unpalatable and unforgivable considering its source—was, after a period of nominal freedom during which his every act was watched, finally handed over to the Nazis for detention. Free, and with his clarion tongue unleashed, he represented too great a danger to the Marshal's dreary concept of order without liberty and to the paralyzing spell which the Marshal's Nazi masters still exercised over the unhappy and benumbed French.

Pierre Laval had been delighted to see Herriot depart. For ten years the brilliant and incorruptible Lyonnais had been strongly disliked by the wily Pierre. The Barthou-Alexander assassination had dealt a final blow to the prestige of the Radical Party. For the next two years there were governments with Radical collaboration but without the party's old-time dominance. The new leaders were for the most part unfamiliar personalities recruited from banking circles and the steel cartel, moderate reactionaries, describing themselves by such meaningless labels as "Republicans of the Left." For Frenchmen generally still revered the liberal tradition too greatly for any aspirant for political honors to dare describe himself openly as a Rightist.

The first of the new cabinets was that of Flandin. It was followed by the return to grace, and to still higher office, of Albert Sarraut. As prime minister, Sarraut was a pitiful front for the activities of the foreign minister, Pierre Etienne Flandin.

Laval and Flandin got along very well together. Their joint interest in the acquisition of power was centered almost entirely in the fortunes it was possible to make through a wise manipulation of foreign policy. The little Socialist lawyer, Laval, had charted his own path shortly after the first World War. Repudiating his electors, he allied himself with the big industrialists and proceeded to cultivate his own material welfare. Almost his first assignment from his new friends was to break up the Russian alliance and to work for a better Franco-German understanding. Re-establishment of German military power seemed for these men the first step toward a new and profitable armaments race. Laval worked well and earned his riches. And finally, as prime minister, he saw his way clear to make millions by dealing not with his former protectors but with his country's enemies.

Mussolini was dreaming at this time of the conquest of

Ethiopia. But he did not dare risk the adventure until he was sure that England and France would not be named as police- men by the League of Nations to put a stop to hostilities and thus serve notice that the rights of weaker nations were still being respected. Il Duce knew that he could not buy a British statesman. But he knew also that England could not act without France. Knowing Laval of old, however, he realized when the astute and rodent-like little lawyer bobbed up as prime minister that now France's neutrality was simply a question of price.

France, of course, did not wish to fight. Had the issues been presented to her as they actually were, undoubtedly she would have fought, particularly if Britain had backed her up. But the British were at the height of their self-delusion as to the real nature of the fascist partners. And France was willing to listen to talk of neutrality in a minor fracas which, after all, was none of her business. The entire so called "patriotic press" upheld Laval in glowing accounts of the friendship of France and Italy and of the "right" of Italy to do in 1935 in Ethiopia what France herself had done in Algeria in 1830.

The argument of course was utterly specious. Apart from the changing concepts of civilization which frowned in this century upon wars of conquest which it had approved a hun- dred years before, there were the signatures of France, and of Italy herself, which were on record in Geneva as being willing to fight for the rights of any small nation attacked by another one. Ethiopia was a League member and was being attacked. But, following the fatal precedent of 1931, when everybody had evaded the implications of the Japanese attack upon Manchuria, France under the direction of Pierre Laval looked the other way when Ethiopia was attacked by her strong and predatory sister nation.

Laval executed his maneuver brilliantly. The British, be-latedly alarmed over the Italian situation, were forced to accept the *fait accompli* handed them by Laval. The Prime Minister himself was able to boast to friends, before whom apparently he was untroubled by any considerations of personal shame, that he had increased his personal holdings by the sum of eighty million francs. He was, moreover, for his strivings in the cause of peace, awarded a pontifical title of nobility.

His fortune made, Count Laval retired with good grace in favor of Pierre Etienne Flandin, to devote his time for the nonce to a continuance of the education in political discontent of Marshal Pétain. He saw, earlier than many, the inevitability of war. He saw too the possible fate of France in such a war, and the role the Marshal might play if defeatism won the day. In grooming the Marshal for his part, he saw how useful to himself the role of indispensable adviser might be. So far Pierre Laval has been a good prophet.

Flandin had been born in somewhat more comfortable circumstances than had the peasant lawyer of Auvergne. He had not had to serve a hard apprenticeship of dirty little jobs in order to win the approval and confidence of the bankers and industrialists. An accomplished business lawyer, he won the attention of men who watched hopefully for just such talents as his, during the Aeropostale trial. Here he and his client and relative, Bouilloux-Lafont, were victorious over enemies more powerful and equally as unscrupulous as they. After this experience he was able to choose his clientele and to the chosen ones he devoted a limitless energy and ambition.

He knew and approved of Laval's deal with Mussolini and he hoped for an opportunity of similar scope. It came.

A poker player of notable talent, Flandin, as Sarraut's foreign minister and strong man, was given a chance to test his inscrutability over Germany's march into the Rhineland. At the time the shortsighted lovers of peace trembled over Hitler's temerity and its possible effect upon the "warlike" French. It was true that at the moment Hitler's strength still was embryonic. Within a few days the French Army could have settled the question and shown the newly ambitious Reich that the Versailles Treaty still had meaning. It has since been wondered whether the master diplomat, Hitler, had weighed the matter of France's rebuff to England over the Ethiopian affair and had counted upon English influence to hold the French still. This may be true, and it is certainly true that English opinion on the whole was not disposed to see the real significance of the Rhineland march. The whole strange and perverted sentimentality of the thirties still strongly swayed the British and made them entirely unable to see that the Germany whose re-emergence as a power they welcomed so benevolently was an entirely different nation from the ill-fated Weimar Republic.

But in the matter of the Rhineland occupation France had no need to wait upon England. This was a matter which could have been settled directly and briefly between France and Germany. That it was not so settled, that Hitler took this daring chance and succeeded with it, was due in the main to the fact that in Flandin the Fuehrer found an instrument to his hand as ambitious and as pliable as Mussolini had found in Laval. The understanding was complete and it extended to the feeble protestations, entirely out of character with the vigor and determination of the man, which were all Flandin could summon to meet the occasion. And after the crucial few days passed without the action which would have ended the matter, Sarraut, who had permitted himself to make a "fighting" speech in which he declared that "France would never permit Strasbourg to come within the range of German guns," had to cool down. But so sure was Hitler that no untoward action would result from his boldness that he had even offered himself as ransom in a curious suicide pact with the German General Staff. Unhappily, thanks to Flandin, the need never arose for the redemption of that pledge.

Sarraut was, it is true, vaguely uncomfortable about the whole affair. But he dared do nothing to cross his indomitable foreign minister. The crisis ended with a few whining speeches, a few complaints about the attitude of England and a smooth pledge from Hitler that now he was satisfied. He would ask for no more concessions from the generous French. And so the French, who had been momentarily disturbed, decided that after all one more little clause in a treaty was not worth the horrors of war.

As for the two principals, Flandin and Hitler, they were well pleased. Indeed, their deal was far more extensive in scope than the Mussolini-Laval bargain. Laval merely sold a country whose continued independent existence was for Europe and France merely a matter of principle. Flandin sold to Hitler the future of his own native land, the possibility of new and more far-reaching aggressions, the beginnings of distrust and mutual suspicion which later were to make his deadly task even more easy. The immediate departure of Belgium from the *Entente Cordiale* was the first tiny straw in the wind. It followed as a direct consequence this seemingly innocent Rhineland venture.

As for the pay-off in this international deal, only rumor has named the sums which changed hands. Flandin, more discreet or perhaps more susceptible to criticism than Laval, has never divulged his share in the business. But rumor in

Switzerland, where the deal was consummated, put the sum at a hundred million Swiss francs. Flandin was known to be expensive, but Germany could afford to pay. She was reaping at the time a golden harvest of credits from the United States and Great Britain, credits which her new rulers knew well they had no intention of paying.

Remember the careers of these two men in connection with their later leadership under the minor Fuehrer of Vichy. The Marshal's first act upon coming to power was to call in his old friend and instructor Pierre Laval as Minister of Foreign Affairs. When the latter's schemes to overreach the Marshal enraged the ancient tyrant and he removed Laval from power, it was Pierre Etienne Flandin upon whom he called to take the vacant office.

At the time of the Rhineland occupation the Marshal was almost completely the prisoner of his admirers. These had seen the betrayal of Ethiopia with satisfaction and had approved the "sensible" conduct of Flandin. Still unwilling to call themselves fascists or openly to admit their sympathies, they applauded every new demonstration of absolute power by the enemies of their country and cleverly put before the Marshal the contrast between fascist order and discipline and the rowdy and inefficient conduct of the democracies. And the Marshal was an avid pupil. Italy had her Mussolini; Germany had her Hitler. Why should not poor, sick France, which so obviously needed a firm and kindly hand, have her Pétain?

CHAPTER 5

WHILE GERMANY CROUCHED
TO SPRING

FOR ALMOST SIXTY-FIVE YEARS the French reactionaries had talked and thought wistfully of the possibility of a *coup d'état*, but not in all that time had it seemed wise or even desirable to foment one, in the absence of any leader who might have unified all the squabbling factions and jealous personalities. But the first few years of the thirties, with their succession of dreary Radical Party scandals and the example, just across the borders, of the success of two strong men were to provide plenty of temptation. It began to seem temptingly easy to take power away from the people, who now did not seem able to use it to their own advantage. Both Hitler and Mussolini had shown how simple the procedure was; one simply bought a few civil servants occupying key positions and a few generals whom the troops would follow, and the thing was done. All the advantages so far had remained in the hands of the plotters.

The time, of course, was particularly opportune for both leaders, as, indeed, it was rapidly coming to be in France. No *coup* will succeed while the people are attached to their leaders and while they have faith in the government of their choice. This, generally speaking, is why democracies may safely permit to malcontents and plotters the degree of lati-

tude they so often do. A regime built upon the will of the
people need not fear so long as it satisfies the people. A
regime built upon force and with the intention of suppressing
the people cannot afford so much as a whisper of discontent.
All facility for the interchange of opinion must be suppressed,
all potential leaders must be imprisoned or massacred and a
constant propaganda against change must be maintained lest
the people stir in their drugged sleep. Only intervention from
without can destroy fascism and its kindred authoritarian
regimes and, as the French reactionaries well knew, the people
themselves will swiftly and effectually overthrow any attempt
at a seizure of power which is not timed to take advantage
of a moment of disorganization or dissatisfaction with popular government.

When Mussolini ordered the March on Rome, his hour
was perfectly chosen. The Italian workers, badly advised by
leaders dizzy in their success and incapable of good judgment,
were committing scattered but regrettable excesses. The occupation of factories, the menacing disturbances of owners and
managers, wild and shameful attacks upon their wives and
daughters, had shocked and puzzled Italian public opinion.
The Rightist press succeeded in thoroughly alarming the
middle classes with the bolshevik bogey and the famous poster
of the Communist with a knife between his teeth was everywhere on display. Mussolini the strong man had come to
restore order, and in the beginning there was merely relief
that somebody was willing to try. The first street brawls, the
whippings, the castor oil publicly forced upon the striking
Socialists, all were accepted as signs that the "Red ghosts"
were meeting their match. By the time the people understood,
it was too late. The day of free discussion was over. A government which could be replaced from inside by the will of

the people had given way to a government safe, apparently for all time, from revolution, since opposition meant civil war and death for the side without arms.

The Nazi method was a little different. The Beer Hall Putsch of 1923 had been ridiculous and abortive. The German people were not yet so deeply disillusioned with the Weimar Republic as they were later to become. But as time passed and the aura of defeat which clung so obstinately to that unhappy experiment in democracy showed no sign of clearing, as the economic crisis settled down to a seeming permanence, the depressed Germans began looking elsewhere for inspiration. They found it in the swagger and bluster of the new political party with its promises of revived military glory to grow from the ashes of defeat, with its contempt for orthodox economics and the general impression of fearless youth it managed to convey through the medium of the several thousand young toughs in whom Hitler drilled a semblance of military order. Instinctively impressed by manifestations of power and unmoved by the mere passivity of righteousness, the German people began to join the new movement. The democrats spoke, and spoke mournfully, while the Nazis marched and recruited.

Nazism, like fascism, was born among frightened and selfish civilians. Their leaders promptly sought agreement with the heads of the armies in order that a counter-revolt should not crush them. It is never difficult to convince the orthodox officer caste, particularly of a defeated or militarily inferior nation, of the national advantages of a strong hand, well reinforced by military might.

In Spain the situation, although nominally reversed, was basically the same. The fascist movement there was almost wholly military in its beginnings but it would have collapsed

in a few weeks without the vehement support of the land-
owners, the wealthy clergy, who for the first time were being
required to pay taxes, and the reactionary middle classes.
And, of course, the implied support of the strong neighbors
who saw, more clearly than the democracies, the usefulness of
a friendly or a paralyzed Spain.

This genesis of our present war began when a handful of
rebel generals landed in Cadiz with a few thousand professional Moorish warriors, happy in the thought of pillaging,
robbing and slaughtering a western land. These were the
people whom the idle, reactionary, parasitic mass of Spaniards
hailed as "saviors" and upon whom they fastened the distinction of being holy warriors. It was sheer accident that
the leader of this movement, San Giurgio, soon lost his life
in an airplane accident, handing over command to the eager
and as yet unknown Francisco Franco.

During these fateful weeks of 1936, France spared little
time for the Spanish upheaval, being herself in the throes of
an election campaign. The Radical Party, which, in spite of
its name was a fairly close approximation of the Democratic
Party in the United States, was beginning now to realize
how drastically it had fallen from grace in the public eye.
It had dominated without interruption—and this, probably,
was one of its major troubles—since 1905, the end of the
Dreyfus Affair. But thirty-one years of power had merely
whetted the appetites of those of its members who refused
to see the wisdom of retirement until the odor of successive
scandals had had time to die. Years of soft jobs, of uninterrupted nepotism, of opportunities for enrichment that
stayed comfortably on the borderland of graft, had spoiled
the party chieftains for impending oblivion. And at this
time it was assiduously looking around for an alliance which

would enable it to assume the mantle of respectability while sacrificing none of the loot of office.

The parties of the Right carefully looked the other way when Radical leaders made a tentative, hopeful approach. They were becoming imbued with a spirit of victory and were ill disposed to cut the incumbents in on it. Furthermore their successful campaign of vilification had been based upon the thesis that the Radicals were the fountainhead of all corruption. They could hardly remain consistent and admit such villains into their councils.

The Socialists had for the Radicals a contempt at least equal to that of the Rightist parties. But they were more amenable. Never having had a taste of power, they were rather pathetically anxious to acquire it. They knew that alone they had no chance of victory at the polls, and they knew also that if the vote were split into too many fragments the Rightists would triumph. And with them could come fascist revolution, perhaps even an extension of Spain's civil war—prospects which held out no hope of peace for France and none for power and expansion among the Socialists. Without enthusiasm, but with reasonably good grace, the Socialists accepted the alliance.

But as the campaign developed, straw polls began to reveal ominous developments. Reactionary strength was greater even than the Radicals and Socialists had feared. Another alliance was necessary unless certain defeat were to be faced. And now the only choice left was the feared but growing Communist Party. The partnership was offered and accepted. And thus the Front Populaire was born.

Much nonsense has been talked about this coalition, much misunderstanding of its aims and achievements has spread outside of France. And one point too often forgotten is that

without this alliance the elections of 1936 almost inevitably
would have resulted in the victory of the Right. The fascist
majority would then have had clear sailing. With their
figurehead President, Marshal Pétain, safely installed, a series
of alliances with Germany, with Italy, with Japan, would
have been imposed upon a people deftly deprived of the
means of resistance. The People's Front defeated this plan
and saved France for a few more years for democracy. Which
is why its leaders, Daladier and Blum, were tried for treason
in the sorry farce at Riom, and why the Communist leader,
Gabriel Peri, was handed over by Pétain's men to be shot as
a hostage by the Nazis.

With a Rightist government in France, committed in
advance to an alliance with Germany, World War II would
have run a different course. With France at his side, Hitler
would have encountered no shadow of opposition in eastern
Europe. England would have found herself confronted with a
fait accompli, as she had once before with Ethiopia. Public
opinion in the United States would have been profoundly
influenced by the impregnability of Hitler's fortress, and the
voices of isolationism would have been strengthened in
their conviction that it would be possible to do business with
a Europe stabilized under Hitler. The Nazification of Europe
and then of the world would have been immeasurably
simplified. With the Popular Front, France too bought
precious time in which the democracies might awaken and
save themselves and the world.

One cheerful feature of the Rightist position was that
without exception the heads of its component parties detested
each other. Their aim was the overthrow of the Republic but
each was determined to accomplish this without permitting
any advantage to accrue to his rivals. None of them had

sufficient prestige or personal magnetism to wean away the partisans of the others. Laval, Flandin, Caillaux, Dc la Rocque, Pozzo di Borgo, Doriot, Taittinger, Daudet, Maurras were unhappy and suspicious as a pack of wolves scenting an inaccessible carcass. The most they could arrange, in face of the Front Populaire combination, was a temporary truce. First they would overthrow the regime and elect Marshal Pétain as the country's titular leader. And then would come the grand battle for spoils. The Marshal was unanimous choice only because his prestige would appeal to all of the simple and undecided souls who could not see behind the façade, and because his advanced age (he was then eighty) meant that nobody need wait very long for the inheritance.

But the People's Front upset the plan and won resoundingly. However, the Radical Party suffered greatly. It had counted upon its subsidiaries to bring in the margin necessary for victory but had supposed that the bulk of its own votes would make possible an amiable condescension and a few sops in the way of minor offices. Instead the Socialists led, and the Communists were almost as numerous as the battered Radicals.

And now for four crucial years the partisans of Pétain were held at bay. This year of stay-in strikes, of the famous forty-hour week and of the other concessions to workers which earned the head-shakings of conservatives the world over was, in its essence, one in which the incumbent government sincerely tried to improve the lot of people who had been forgotten in the spoilsmen's rush of earlier cabinets. The strikes were curious. They broke out, at the instigation of mysterious agitators, against the wishes, the interest and the orders of the trades union leaders themselves. The worst of them occurred in the month following the elections which

preceded the actual assumption of power by the new government. They might, even then, so strong was the state of
French feeling during the whole of this campaign, have led
to bloodshed, even to civil war, had the intentions of their
perpetrators been fulfilled. But the quiet good sense and
patriotism of Léon Blum settled a tense problem within a
comparatively short time.

Social reform was the avowed aim of the Blum government.
The reproach has been made that the reforms were badly
timed, but not even the most bitter reactionary could with
justice say that they were not long overdue. Even the forty-
hour week, which has been freely blamed for many of France's
troubles, made at that time little or no difference to armaments production since the economic crisis and the par-
simoniousness of three preceding Ministers of War (Pétain,
Maurin, Fabry) had combined to cut armaments appropria-
tions to the bone with the result that practically no worker
in France had a guaranteed work week of so much as thirty
hours. The Popular Front's government appropriated sums of
money unheard of for armaments—fourteen billion francs!

Léon Blum, an honest, sensitive and conscientious public
servant, has been blamed without reason for mistakes which
he inherited or which arose from the times and the circumstances in which he assumed office. He was not the only
one who paid heed to the Fuehrer's protestations of love
and peace. Preceding French cabinets and the two Conservative prime ministers of England also had swallowed the bait
with the eagerness of wishful thinking. Furthermore Blum's
scrupulous honesty made him lean over in an effort at courtesy
to Germany. Since he was a Jew and Germany was anti-
Semitic he would permit no man to think that he was putting
the grudge of race ahead of the interest of his country.

The same division of feeling arose to plague him over the Spanish war. As a Socialist, he felt that in all honesty he could not call upon all Frenchmen to fight for the Socialists of Barcelona. And so he permitted himself to be enmeshed in the tragic absurdities of nonintervention, without in any way advancing the real international interests of France. A Loyalist victory would have done much to check the rising prestige of the dictators. Had it been achieved with the aid of France it would have revived the waning confidence of France's smaller allies. Above all, the defeat of Franco and his allies would have meant that France would share with a friendly and grateful Spanish Republic the important boundary of the Pyrenees. Instead, the war in 1939 found France forced to immobilize an army of two hundred thousand men in fear of the tricks of El Caudillo, who might at any moment have decided to follow the back-stabbing tactics of his Italian friend and patron.

It is bitterly ironical that Blum should have faced in the dock at Riom the charge of having thrown France into war. If this unhappy man has any need for self-reproach it is only that he did not force the war in 1936, before the Anschluss, Munich and the Siegfried Line, and while France was still stronger than the expanding Germany, while Mussolini was still recuperating from his Ethiopian adventure and while Russia and Czechoslovakia wished nothing more than French help in destroying the growing Nazi menace. Léon Blum, devoured by scruples, did not dare to bring about war then. But neither had any of his predecessors—and their motives were less worthy than his. After the dishonesty of the clever, France had to endure the weakness of the honest.

The first cabinet of the People's Front had immediately run into trouble. Apart from the tangle of foreign affairs, its

domestic reforms did not please the still predominantly reactionary Senate. The majority in the Chamber of Deputies
was amenable, but two thirds of the Senators were hold-overs
from the previous election.

It was the chairman of the Senate Finance Commission,
the amnestied traitor Joseph Caillaux, who succeeded in up-
setting the Blum Cabinet. This was hailed as a victory by the
money-conscious classes and they had no objection to the
despised and dangerous Chautemps once more returning to
office as prime minister. Léon Blum, with some relief, retired
to the background as vice premier.

In the meantime the venal Rightist press was back at work,
dividing public opinion, stoking the fires for civil war or for
any disorder that might advance their cause. The building of
the Manufacturers' Association was destroyed by a bomb. "A
Communist stroke!" shrieked the Rightists. "Another Reich-
stag fire," retorted the Leftist press.

Public opinion, however, did not fail to note that the ex-
plosion occurred at an hour when none of the wealthy industrialists supposedly menaced were in or near the building. Investigation disclosed not one but two groups of
Rightist plotters, acting in collusion. There was the *Comité
d'Action anti-Revolutionnaire* and the more famous and
sinister *Cagoule*. Following the trail of these two organizations, the investigators made horrifying discoveries of caches
of arms, some from Germany, some from Italy, some from the
very arsenals of the Republic itself. A check-up revealed that
truly enormous quantities of ammunition destined for national
defense had been diverted by the plotters. Powerful industrialists were arrested, and these in turn implicated the
officers responsible for the munitions reserves. These betrayed

others, and gradually the net widened to take in colonels
and even generals. Finally the plot definitely implicated the
head of the army himself, the remaining marshal of France,
the man sworn to uphold the honor and dignity of the Republic by force of arms.

Pétain's connection with the reactionary parties was well
known at this time, although his name had appeared in none
of the 1936 elections. Léon Blum, as head of the winning
party and vice premier, was in position to arrest, to crush
and ruin the old man, to charge and convict him of treason.

He did not do it. . . . With a supreme and fatal magnanimity he declined to shadow the few remaining years of an old
man's life with so grave a charge. His own personal reward
is well known. He was imprisoned with the first grant of
power made to the Vichy government and handed over by
the Marshal without compunction to long imprisonment and
the possibility of torture, and further hounded by the cruel
mockery of a trial which had no ends of justice in view but
was designed only to blacken the characters of those who had
no power or hope of adequate defense. Furthermore he committed the future of France to this same old man who years
earlier had been judged too old to be blamed for treason!

In the end all of the accused were released. Had they not
been, they would have dragged in the name of the Marshal
and his further protection would have been impossible. Besides, so many officers were implicated that nothing short of
a complete purge would have cleared the army of its plotters.
And the clouds of war had gathered too thickly for any such
drastic action. With the honest temporizing of Blum and the
shrewd planning of Chautemps, the decision was taken that
the army should be cleaned, man by man, of its reactionary

elements. But the time that remained was too short, and war caught up with an army in which far too many commanding officers were not at all averse to fascist victory.

But Chautemps was to retire mysteriously within a few months, notwithstanding his previous passion for office. His departure coincided rather curiously with Hitler's overnight annexation of Austria, and the explanation most generally accepted was that, having had advance knowledge of Hitler's intention to march into Austria, Chautemps preferred to have none of the complications of officeholding in France at the time the disclosure was made. So it came about that during the week-end of the annexation France was without a government. And then all of the responsibility for handling the nation through that crucial period fell back upon the unhappy, conscience-tortured, vacillating Léon Blum. During the weeks that followed he suffered also from the blame liberally apportioned to the muddle of international mistakes previously made by Chautemps. This second Blum Cabinet lasted for only a few weeks. Again it fell under assault from the Senate.

Edouard Daladier, since June 1936, War Minister and chief of the now moribund Radical Party, next assumed the premiership. Since the riots of February 1934 and the bloodshed on the Place de la Concorde, Daladier had not succeeded in living down the nickname of "Le Fusilleur", relentlessly kept alive by the fascist press. But now the Rightists were glad to support him as the lesser of two evils, since they realized that the fall of his cabinet would bring the return of still another Socialist as prime minister. For the ugly tag of "Man of the Firing Squad" they substituted the bluff and jovial-sounding "Bull of Vaucluse." Daladier strove valiantly to live up to this somewhat theatrical implication of forthright tenacity but events soon showed one nickname to be about as inapposite as the other.

Daladier availed himself of Rightist help with some thankfulness since it offered a means of escape from the now constant demands of the Communists. However, the switch meant that the titular leader of the Leftist parties in actuality had their interests less and less at heart. Inevitably he began to lose the support of both Communists and Socialists and to recreate his new majority with the aid of the parties which had suffered defeat.

This meant, of course, that he was increasingly unable to refuse anything to his new allies. He was forced to accept, and to make the country accept, the policy of nonintervention in the second phase of the Spanish war, when German and Italian intervention had become so flagrant and it was obvious that without the aid of France the Loyalist cause was doomed. During his entire premiership this elected leader of the People's Front carried out a policy toward Spain in direct contradiction to that demanded by his electorate. All Leftist voters in France were clamoring for the support of the Spanish Republic. But Blum's actual parliamentary supporters were determined to do nothing which would hinder the victory of Franco, and Marshal Pétain was one of the Cabinet's most insistent warners against the danger of involving France in war with a foreign power, thus at the same time running a risk of inflaming the incipient civil war at home.

However, French public opinion was becoming clamorous on the subject of aid to Spain, and Daladier, who was on the side of the people in this, was strongly tempted to send two "unofficial" divisions to the aid of Barcelona. These would have been sufficient to change the balance of power, while a naval demonstration off the Italian coast might have persuaded Mussolini that in this case there might be advantages in combining practical with theoretical neutrality. It should be remembered that at this point the French Army was still the most powerful in Europe.

Daladier now was strongly tempted to throw overboard the advice and support of his Rightist colleagues. But Communist and Socialist suspicions of his vacillations were thoroughly aroused and hard to dispel. So the Bull consulted Pétain and Weygand and their advice settled his doubts. The two reactionaries, in complete agreement, absolutely refused to send fifty thousand men to save Spain on the terms originated by Italy and Germany. They insisted first upon a general mobilization, a move generally accepted as tantamount to a declaration of war, and one sure to result in a matching mobilization of the Axis armies. The dispatch of fifty thousand troops in this defiant fashion would of course have amounted to open warfare, and the blame, as the generals shrewdly foresaw, would have been France's for being the first to mobilize. Daladier was not ready to plunge the continent of Europe into declared war for the sake of Barcelona, and so the French people watched with mingled emotions the death throes of the Spanish Republic.

The triumphant Franco was never thereafter to show any gratitude for this reluctant neutrality on the part of France. He demonstrated instead an arrogance and contempt which grew in proportion to the growing weakness of France. Here again a comment of Clemenceau's applies with depressing force:

"How are we to account," he demanded in 1930, "for these sudden changes? A country subject to sudden bursts of energy in the cause of progress or sunk in the depths of neurasthenia! These excesses cost more than the nation realizes."

By now Daladier was ostentatiously the protégé of Pétain and his circle. The General Staff benevolently permitted this "most Rightist of the Leftists" to acquire the reputation of a military expert. "Daladier has the confidence of the generals" became one of those mystic slogans conferring a special power upon their subjects, and in this instance it was responsible for maintaining Daladier in the post of Minister of Defense for three years. It took the disaster of Sedan, and the consequent humiliation of the generals, whose confidence he so enjoyed, to enable Reynaud to remove him from this post.

In daily conversations the Marshal demonstrated to his new disciple the advantages of defense strategy à la Pétain and the resultant inconsequentiality of any further development in German offensive power.

To this myopic viewpoint the conquest of Austria, the occupation of Memel, the growing hysteria and agitation among the Sudetens were trifles. Her alliances to the east, however, represented potential danger. France, isolated behind her Maginot Line, was not in any particular need of these allies. Far more useful would be the friendship of the new powers, Hitler, Mussolini and Franco, and to the cultivation of these, declared the Marshal, it would be wise for Daladier to devote his energies. Daladier now knew that he had lost the favor of those who had elected him and that the next elections would spell his political end. He therefore joined the ranks of the self-justifiers and decided to prove to the nation that with him the war which loomed ever more menacingly across the skyline could be exorcised.

Thus the tragedy and anticlimax of Munich, with the

immense psychological defeat it entailed for both France and England, was a personal victory for Daladier himself. Had Hitler remained satisfied then, had he not determined to exceed in 1939 all limits imposed by reason, the elections of 1940 would have been a complete triumph for Daladier and the Munich men.

It was not alone a blindness to the shape of things to come that thus influenced France's will to peace. The war of 1914–18 had cost France 1,500,000 dead men, 2,800,000 permanently crippled. The same percentage of affliction would have meant for the United States five million killed and nine million disabled. A lack of abstract enthusiasm for war is understandable under such circumstances, particularly when a powerful press is trumpeting that national honor can be preserved without war and that only invasion can justify further bloodshed. And so Daladier, having abandoned an ally of France, having lost her last chance to beat an ever more menacing foe, having sacrificed her traditional role as a great power in Europe, was greeted with flowers and cheers by the people whom he had doomed.

It is not difficult to understand Daladier's motives and his shortsightedness. Those of his adviser, the Marshal, are more complex. Pétain had a noble and an ignoble motive for preferring peace to war. First he shared the genuine horror of all Frenchmen for further conflict and bloodshed. But he also realized that a new war would be a war of younger generals, a ghostly phalanx of future marshals of France whose glory would eclipse his as already in the minds of the young the glory of a MacArthur, an Eisenhower, must eclipse the fame of a Pershing. He retained an obstinate longing to be the only conqueror.

Furthermore his fear of the possibilities of a Communist

uprising, so assiduously fostered by his friends, was genuine enough. He felt sure that, whichever side was victor, the Communist revolt would come, in Germany or Italy if they were defeated, in England or France if they suffered defeat or a stalemate. But he did not seriously believe, in 1938, that France would be defeated; therefore he was convinced that war would wish upon the states whose discipline he admired the horrors of communism and disorder. In such case, he reasoned, France would in effect have fought a war for the benefit of Moscow, which would be intolerable. And so it seemed that if war must be fought, which was not at all inevitable, it would be best to fight so as not to crush Germany and the excellent government for which she stood. The possibility of France herself being crushed by Germany seemed remote and fantastic to this determinedly one-track mind. The Maginot Line loomed large and comforting, insurance against every possible type of military eventuality, a vast concrete spiderweb in which France needed only to sit and bide her time.

The British and French fleets did, it is true, enter into these calculations as additional insurance. And also the thought had become somewhat recurrent of late that Hitler had developed rather a faculty for making a nuisance of himself. So when the bogey of war did present itself with unusual realism, the thought was there that if it did have to come perhaps it would be possible somewhere in the process to rid Germany of Hitler while preserving his admirable rule of order, and to substitute for him one or other of the strong generals for which the German Army is famous. A military government would be pleasing and seemly and would, moreover, offer a useful precedent.

One other motive found a place in the Marshal's schemes.

True to type, he had become a shrewd and cautious, although small, investor. Even an uneasy peace is to be preferred by such men to the violent oscillations of the stock market produced by war. The Marshal was an old man and had never been a gambler. He did not now fancy entrusting his savings to the unpredictabilities of war.

There was another side to all of this plotting and scheming: the side of France's relations with Russia. Prior to Munich, Russia had vainly tried to induce England and France to aid in the defense of Czechoslovakia. The Russians were ready to intervene at once. Had the three then acted in concert, had war come in 1938 instead of a year later, what would the situation have been? First, Hitler would have backed down. He would have known, through his go-between Bonnet whether or not his bluff would have been called.

Second, Germany was a nation of sixty-five million and was not then armed to the peak of perfection she achieved a year later. She would have been forced to fight in the east against Russia, in the south against the Czechs, in the west against the French and British. She could have been crushed It is sufficient to see what the Russians accomplished in 1942–43, without allies, without a second-front diversion, to see what Germany's fate might have been in a war for the liberty of Czechoslovakia. And these were considerations which should have seemed elementary to the Marshal, the senior strategist of Europe at that time. Furthermore Mussolini remembering his old role as champion of the independence of Austria, undoubtedly would have joined the conquerors as soon as it was prudent to do so. Franco, exhausted by three years of civil war and abruptly deprived of his nonintervening allies, would have been glad to make peace with Barcelona and to escape with his life. And above all, two million magnificent Czech soldiers with their five armored divisions would have fought Germany in 1938 instead of being forced to fight for her under the swastika two years later.

The difference, a year later, was that Germany was able to throw into the war ten armored divisions against three and a half French. Before Munich she would have had to oppose five panzer divisions to eight and a half Franco-Czechs' plus the Russians'. After Munich the huge balance of the Czech armies and equipment, plus the huge Skoda factories in Bohemia, were thrown against any democratic alliance.

Only the obstinate blindness of a Pétain, a Daladier, a Chamberlain, could have refused to face such elementary arithmetic as this. Stalin soon understood that he could in no way rely upon support from the west in case of conflict with Germany. His information service at this time was reportedly the best in Europe and it kept him fully informed of the Anglo-French intrigues conducted in the hope of engaging Germany and Russia in a war of extermination. But being shrewder by far than the plotters, he had no intention of permitting Russia to fight alone against Germany for the satisfaction of nations which were afraid of both. He understood that Russia's fate in such a situation might well be that of the Spanish Republic, which had had kind words, crocodile tears and not a vestige of practical help in its long death agony just concluded.

But the summer of 1939, following the march on Prague which had at last shaken some of the complacency from Daladier and Chamberlain, saw a reluctant change of tactics. The insulting conferences of Munich, from which Russia was so pointedly excluded, were forgotten, and Russia at last was wooed by the nations which had treated her heretofore with such marked disdain. But Stalin, the supreme opportunist, had not been idle. Neither had Hitler and his assistant, Von Ribbentrop. Hitler's immediate plans required a Russia immobilized at least temporarily. He had sent Von Ribbentrop to the Kremlin well equipped with dictaphone records of conservations between the champagne salesman and the ambassadors of France and England which effectively revealed the naïve verbal offers of neutrality made by representatives of both countries in case they could bring about this long-hoped-for struggle between the Nazi tiger and the Soviet bear.

But it was not alone the record of a duplicity too transparent to be very deceptive that took Stalin into the famous nonaggression pact of the summer of 1939. He saw now that war was inevitable for England and France unless they intended an intolerable submission to further and still further German demands, and this the rising temper of the people of both countries rendered increasingly improbable. He saw no reason why he should now allay their growing fears by conciliating people who had shown themselves so notably unconciliatory toward him. Together with Germany he sprang the nonaggression pact upon a stupefied world in the expectation that a resistant Europe would engage Germany in a bitter war of attrition which he would enter in his own good time, reserving the right to dominate the peace as the eleventh-hour savior of Europe.

BOOK TWO

●

THE HOW

CHAPTER 6

FRANCE'S LAST MILE

As BASIC AND TAKEN-FOR-GRANTED a postulate as her relationship with England had been France's attitude toward her Russian alliance for many years prior to August 1939. It had seemed inevitable that, in the unwelcome eventuality of a new war with Germany, Russia would be fighting with the French. Furthermore the theatrical enmity of the two totalitarian nations had impressed Frenchmen with a sense of their utter irreconcilability. For this reason the "realism" of Pierre Laval had made some headway. Since Russia under no circumstances could be a friend of Germany, why should France tie herself to aid Russia in any war that giant might feel called upon to try its strength upon? Better, perhaps, to withdraw from formal alliances and trust to the logic of circumstance which ordained that France had no enemy but Germany and that in the event of attack from this quarter Russia in her own defense would automatically come to the rescue.

Thus the Russo-German pact was a blow to the heart of every Frenchman. The country now began to see the reality behind those long, cold shadows that closed in from every side. Suddenly the line-up, which before Munich had looked so favorable, became extraordinarily ominous. The military might of Czechoslovakia had been bartered away for a scrap of paper. Russia, incredibly, had taken her innumerable troops into the opposite camp. There was no sign that in this fast-approaching war Italy or even Japan would be upon the side of France. And finally Spain, which had been held from 1914–18 in the strictest neutrality through the efforts of King Alfonso, was now a new and menacing threat. Far from showing any gratitude for the French neutrality which had insured his victory, Franco lost no opportunity to voice his contempt and dislike for the democracies, his admiration and imitation of his powerful Axis protectors.

The French General Staff now had real and urgent preoccupations. Formerly the problem had consisted in bringing Germany to her senses through the disposition of a huge coalition of force, without crushing her to the point of encouraging the dreaded communist revolution. Now, France, without allies excepting England, who, as everybody knew, would not be fully prepared at least until 1941, and Poland with her peerless armies and courage but handicapped by the dubious leadership of Colonel Beck, had to revise these vague hopes of crushing Germany with kid gloves. The question now was how to mark time, how to temporize until England could be ready, until some as yet unplanned miracle would bring streams of munitions from the United States and tip the scales once again in France's favor.

Among the frantic last-minute expedients was a half-hearted wooing of Italy in the hope of extracting a promise of at least conditional neutrality, and a sudden assiduous courting of the swaggering Franco.

A plan to win some slightly more friendly attitude from Franco had begun as early as March 1939, when the first straws had begun to show which way the wind might blow. The emissary chosen to try to charm the stand-offish

Caudillo was none other than Marshal Pétain. Who could possibly be a more flattering ambassador than he, the venerable hero, a devotee of the same brand of clerico-fascism as Franco himself, and an old friend and campaigner of the new master of starving Spain? Nobody, in the eyes of the French people, was better qualified to bring about a better understanding with Spain than this old and wise man. It was merely a matter of sitting back and waiting for the warm winds of friendship to begin wafting in from the south.

But public opinion was in for a rude shock. Not only did Franco not receive this venerable emissary with flattered surprise; he refused for weeks to receive him at all. For Franco, very much on his dignity with the Daladier government, had transmitted a flat demand for the gold deposited by the Barcelona government with the Bank of France, and also for the return of those ships of the Spanish fleet still interned at Bizerte. There had been an understandable reluctance on the part of the French thus to seal their recognition of the new Spanish regime, although they had authorized the slightly less official gesture of sending a friendly emissary. However, the victorious Franco was adamant. His old friend the Marshal was forced to cool his heels at Hendaye until the French agreed to capitulate.

Once the little matters of the gold and the fleet were straightened out, Franco was disposed to receive somewhat more graciously the old man whose ideas were in essence so similar to his own. When he recrossed the Pyrenees, the French ambassador to Spain was secretly transformed into the *chargé d'affaires* of the Axis. Interesting testimony to his frame of mind at this time and later, after France finally was involved in her war of survival, comes from one of the most alert and objective of American foreign correspondents,

H. R. Knickerbocker, whose recent book, *Is Tomorrow Hitler's?* includes this anecdote:

"I have personally been able to verify conclusively the fact that Marshal Pétain, having invited two highly placed Spaniards to dine with him in Hendaye in November 1939, said to his guests:

" 'Do not judge France by its present appearance. Democracy is finished everywhere. Next spring will see a movement in France comparable to your own national uprising.'

"Such a phrase in the mouth of a French ambassador who was at the same time a French military leader was extremely significant. What other meaning could a revolt in wartime have except that its intent was to end the war? What other reason could there have been for waiting until spring except that this period was the best for a German offensive?"

In the atmosphere of Burgos the old soldier saw a literal realization of his hazy dreams of many years. Here was the ex-Colonel Franco of the old days of the Riff wars, a Franco who had succeeded in doing what the most distinguished survivor of the earlier World War had longed, but hesitated, to attempt. Through force and only through force, made impregnable by the support of powerful friends, he had been able to impose his inflexible rule upon Spain, to bring about this "order" which has seemed to so many military martinets the quality most worth imposing upon the civilian scene.

For almost an entire year Franco demonstrated to the Marshal—who desired nothing so much as to be convinced—the advantages of a strong hand over a nation which had seceded from the severer virtues of order and the quasi-military religion revered by the clerico-fascists. Here Pétain found emphatic support for his conviction that the decadent Third Republic deserved to disappear. He found also a

shrewdly sympathetic understanding of his long-standing
grievances, of the fact that only when France was in mortal
danger had the Republic deigned to ask his advice and aid.
At Verdun, in Champagne, at the *Chemin des Dames* and
again in Morocco, his had been the presence that made
victory possible. Only by consenting to be pilloried in the
Doumergue Cabinet had he, single-handed, averted from
the luckless politicians of the Republic the fury of the people.
Now, again, he was stepping into the breach, was winning
for a nation that did not deserve it the friendship of a Spain
revitalized by the strength of his friend, El Caudillo Franco.

Franco was indeed the Marshal's friend, but it was the
friendship of Mephistopheles for the querulous old Faust. It
was Franco who suggested, no doubt according to directions
from his own more powerful friends, the plan at which the
Marshal was hinting in his conversations with the Spanish
friends which Mr. Knickerbocker reported. Shorn of much
tortuous approach and self-justification, the plan probably
followed this outline:

It was possible that one day again in the near future the
French armies might find themselves in trouble. And then,
no doubt, it would be Marshal Pétain who would once more
be called upon to rescue them. The situation would be somewhat similar to that of 1917, when the military situation plus
growing domestic mutterings persuaded the parliamentarians
to relinquish the authority they had guarded so jealously
into the temporary possession of their most formidable
representative, Georges Clemenceau. But this time the
Marshal would be France's Clemenceau and he was to accept,
at first with due modesty, the dictatorial powers thus con-
ferred. But once full power was in his hands he was not to
wait until danger had passed, as Clemenceau did, only to find

himself dropped by a resurgent Parliament. He was to upset
the Republic there and then, using the emergency to delay a promised plebiscite. Then the authoritarian regime
France so badly needed could be established on a firm
foundation. Hitler, who was so admirable an authoritarian
himself and who possessed so profound an admiration for
the Marshal, would be most happy to aid so desirable a
dénouement as the establishment of order in unhappy France,
and the war, which would from then on be motiveless, would
come to an end with Europe, purged and recreated, happily
unified under the New Order.

The Marshal's long susceptibility to flattery had been
strengthened by age. He was by now utterly incapable of an
objective examination of so preposterous a suggestion.
Furthermore the trouble clouds were now too large to be
ignored, and even the colossal self-esteem of the Marshal
was suffering from vague doubts as to the wisdom of the
course upon which he had planted the feet of France.

It is a matter of opinion as to just where and when France
lost the war of 1940. It is partly true that it was lost at
Munich. It also is partly true that it was lost when France
reacted so supinely to the insolent violation of the Versailles
Treaty embodied in the Rhineland occupation. But it also
is equally true in another sense that France lost the war of
1940 even before the start of the war of 1914. She lost it in
some measure in the far-off years of 1907-08, when Major-
Professor Pétain and Brigadier General-Dean Foch argued
with cold politeness their theories of warfare in the dusty classrooms of L'Ecole Supérieure de Guerre.

For the great offensive-defensive argument which began
then may be simplified even further into a contest between
the admirers of two weapons, with all of the vast psycho-

logical cleavage the advocacy of those weapons implies. For Pétain it was the machine gun, that compact tool of death with which one installs oneself in a handy trench and waits for the enemy foolhardy enough to attack. For Foch it was the bayonet, the weapon of attack which does not wait for an enemy but rushes out to seek him.

The machine gun had been invented in 1895 and it was still a controversial weapon in the days when the cleavage between the two teachers was widening irreparably. It made no great appeal to the advocates of bayonet warfare, but to students of the tactics of defense its advantages were manifold and immediately apparent.

Pétain in those days had the courage of his too rigid convictions. He concentrated upon the machine gun with the same single-minded intensity General Billy Mitchell was later to devote to airplane warfare and which General de Gaulle gave to the study of mechanized war. He headed a school for machine-gun training at Camp Châlons in 1902, and everything in his studies combined to convince him that the machine gun would dominate the battlefield of the future.

The higher rank of Foch, who though incomparably the greater soldier was not the most tactful superior officer in the world, permitted him to silence his subordinate without effecting any change in Pétain's convictions. And the first years of World War I appeared strikingly to justify Machine-gun-Pétain's point of view, even to the point of making Bayonet-Foch his subordinate. But the Marshal was never to learn that defense alone cannot win a war. The last months of 1917 and the rest of the war were won by the tactics of attack and by the aid of the tanks which were to acquire over the machine gun the same superiority that this weapon a little earlier had assumed over the bayonet.

The experience might have proved to a younger, more liberal-minded man the necessity of a more diversified viewpoint upon tactics. It was to have no such effect upon Pétain. Stubbornly he maintained that the brilliant successes of Foch were a matter of luck and injustice which basically proved nothing. The death of Foch was to him the long-awaited opportunity to prove, if need be with the entire French Army, the superiority of the machine gun, the inevitable, patient triumph of defensive war.

And so, since 1929, the Marshal had prepared his war of defense, for only a successful defensive war would demonstrate and prove irrevocably his long rightness. Furthermore in theory he was not averse to a strong enemy, since against a weak one no conclusive demonstration would be possible. Hence there were two reasons why he did not wish to interfere in the Rhineland occupation and the continued strengthening of the German Army. First it would have meant an attack, and an attack of superior force. And again, 1936 was the honeymoon of the Nazi regime, the time when many of its earlier admirers of order and the strong hand had not yet been frightened away by the naked brutality of the real thing. An attack in 1936 would, it is true, have scotched, maybe killed, the growing military pretensions of the fascist partners. But it would also have meant handing Germany back to communist revolution or perhaps to another struggle to establish democratic government, and this was not a step Pétain or his backers had been disposed to insist upon. Furthermore—and this was a consideration more personal to Pétain—such a victory would have proved the rightness of the Foch theories and would have left the old apostle of the defensive probably for the rest of his life in the position of a man who had devoted a lifetime to the wrong theories.

So that Pétain, in this strange dream period before Munich, was not ill disposed toward a large and growing German Army. And even Munich did not arouse him, since his megalomania made it easy for him to decide that a battle in which Russia, England and Czechoslovakia all fought with France would not make for the resounding all-French triumph which he felt that the next war might well produce. In addition, by waiting just a little longer, France might well be the attacked, not the attacker, and then in short order she could toss the invader back from her borders without so overwhelming an array of help.

But now, in the summer of 1939, the whole situation had somehow changed. As Kaiser Wilhelm had muttered a quarter of a century before, so Pétain now echoed: "I did not want this." Germany had grown not only strong but practically indomitable. And while there might be some glory in a single-handed victory with Russia waiting to spring to France's aid in the event of some untoward happening, purchasing the same glory with Russia, cold and menacing, now upon the other side, seemed incomparably more expensive and difficult. As much as any of his countrymen the Marshal had relied upon the inevitability of a Russian alliance, and without it the task facing France in a world of steel spikes seemed formidable indeed. But there is always a crumb of comfort and this time it was that the initiative was now taken out of the hands of France. No hot-head would now overrule him and send the country plunging into a disastrous offensive. The odds were too great. And certainly, if defense could win this time, it would be a triumph for the Marshal worthy of a permanent niche in the annals of strategy.

These were not necessarily matters for the ear of Franco, since all plotters must keep a portion of their own counsel.

But Franco may well have pointed out with elaborate tact that the dark days of retreat which any defensive war necessitates are just the sort of days that produce from the people a cry for stronger direction, for a firm hand at the top.

It is very necessary to try to understand the tangle of cross-purposes, of doubts and hopes, that beset the mind of this very old man during the last months of 1939. He had no personal or ideological hatred of Hitler and Mussolini. Indeed it seemed to him merely an unfortunate accident that they should now be warring with France, and one which he hoped could be concluded without damaging a very real potential friendship. He felt that with their help it was now imminently possible to rid France of her real enemies, the parliamentary parasites, the strange Communist and Radical agitators who had clamored so loudly during the past few years.

For the greater part of his life he had remained a soldier, pure and simple. Actually a normal life span had ended for him when he began to interest himself seriously in politics. But this new ambition (and it was one which had lain dormant in a naturally authoritarian mind) soon came to rival, if not eclipse, his earlier dreams of someday being known as France's greatest soldier. And somewhere in this conflict of two ambitions a simple and instinctive patriotism had withered and died. For the greater part of his life the Marshal had put France first, had identified his honor with hers. And then, insensibly almost, his irritation with the politicians, his admiring envy of other strong men, his quite sincere conviction of France's need for a firm hand, and above all the endless and poisoning flattery of powerful and traitorous sycophants, began to accomplish their deadly work. Following the February riots, the Marshal found himself, perhaps with out his own realization at first, increasingly more of a Rightist partisan, less of a French patriot. The new school of thought which parroted of the "haves" and the "have-nots," which spoke of discipline and the master races, and of the decadence of the old democracies, had in him a fascinated convert. And of all countries France was the least susceptible to such doctrines—France, which had practically no "have-nots," which gloried in her lack of discipline and which granted to every race within her jurisdiction, black and white alike, the same opportunities, the same human respect.

For this war now beginning the French people had little enthusiasm. They had been restrained from fighting when their energies and their convictions alike had clamored for a part in the Spanish war; and again when Austria, which from old ties of friendship and sympathy they loved and pitied, had been overrun. They had been willing, too, to fight beside the Czechs, for here French honor was involved. But now apparently they must fight for Poland, which of late years had been neither a tractable European neighbor nor a notable opponent of Axis ideas. France did not forget that at the time of the Czech dismemberment Poland's Colonel Beck had not only upheld all German claims but had clamored for a share of the plunder.

And so France did not go to war for the sake of Poland but rather because at last people and government alike realized with a dreary finality that the tragedy of twenty-five years before was about to be re-enacted and that once more it was necessary to fight Germany or to be swallowed. But they could see now, with the tragic clarity of hindsight, that in 1936 victory would have been easy; that in 1938 it would have been sure, if more expensive, and that now it was almost too late. Why should they fight now when it was to be a long

and difficult ordeal, draining still more of the lifeblood of
France away? Only from desperation and a sense that events
had outstripped them. As a man who has gangrene may object
to the removal of his toe, so France had balked at war in
1936. And as the same man, frightened but still refusing to
face reality, with the disease advanced now to his knee, France
again faltered in 1938. And now there was no longer room for
doubt or hope. The leg must be amputated at the waist and
without even the certitude this time of a happy outcome.

The cumbersome preparations were under way. But none
of them were adequate for, or had been devised for, a war in
which France must face the enemy alone until Great Britain
should come to her aid. All of the maps and blueprints, the
orders on what to do when mobilization came, had been
based upon the certainty that Russia also would be an ally
of France. And what, together with Russian strength, would
still have seemed a fair superiority began to look strangely
little and lonely when viewed as the major resource.

One might have thought that the persistent policy of insult
to Russia which had been pursued unchecked for years by
Pierre Laval and his clique and the Rightist press in general
would have caused some Frenchmen to wonder whether
France herself might not repudiate this alliance and therefore
prepare to meet war alone. Not only, however, had France
not done this, but now, even in the eleventh hour, now that
the Russians had gone and the British had warned of the
time it might take them to prepare, the nation still seemed
paralyzed. No superhuman effort galvanized the whole nation
into activity. Instead France sat supine behind the Maginot
Line, with a faith in the Marshal and the army and a pathetic
wishfulness to believe in the whole fabric of foolish and useful
fables of a "war of attrition" that the press of both France

and England were guilty at this time of pouring out to their bewildered readers.

As a result of the Marshal's preoccupation with defensive strategy, and the complete incomprehension of the French General Staff of the terrible juggernaut now facing them, France had given only a minor percentage of its effort and funds to the provision of planes and tanks. The Polish campaign was a cruel awakening. Some of the younger military men, less obstinate and more alert to the potential disasters of defeat, began pleading for stronger aviation support and better equipped motorized divisions. But nothing happened. No orders were placed at this time for American steel, and tank production was limited to the small available stock of French steel, most of which had to come from Lorraine, soon to be under heavy German gunfire.

Nothing was done to insure adequate supplies of American duralumin, so indispensable to plane production. French purchasing missions in the United States made the tragic error of placing their orders for airplanes with the two big American companies having large priority orders for the United States government, while idle and waiting factories received no orders. And this was only a few months before Paul Reynaud's unforgettable appeal begged for "planes, clouds of planes!" As though planes could be manufactured overnight like loaves of bread.

Still worse, a steady inefficiency which came close to being, and may in fact have been, calculated sabotage, delayed and rendered useless many an American airplane that might otherwise have given useful service. Shipments, for instance, almost never arrived complete. One ship would carry a consignment of wings to Casablanca. Another would bring all motors and deliver them at another port, hundreds of miles away. Several hundred planes remained agonizingly on the ground during the worst need of 1940 because no generators had been provided for them. Others were idle because the ships carrying their propellers had been torpedoed. This was a terrible time in which to learn that a plane "nearly" complete is equivalent to no plane at all.

An important factor in the hindrance and inefficiency which hampered France to the end was the attitude of the big French industrialists. They did not believe in a long or a dangerous war. After the first reverses, they thought, their leader, Marshal Pétain, would assume complete control, would hasten peace negotiations on terms favorable to an authoritarian France, and then everybody could resume business as usual. It seemed to them far more important not to risk a congestion of world markets, a crisis of overproduction and an encouragement of a host of small and ambitious competitors than it did to stimulate at once the tremendous output of arms and machines necessary for a desperate war. Their state of mind is not so dissimilar after all from that of the British and American rubber speculators who deprecated all warnings, in the year or two before Pearl Harbor, that a war in the Pacific would seriously jeopardize the world's natural rubber supply and who therefore fought with all of the powerful weapons at their command both the building of adequate stock piles and the development of a synthetic rubber industry which might have given theoretical competition to their monopoly.

Furthermore there was not the financial interest in this war that there had been in earlier, more profitable encounters. In every country—in the democracies from popular demand, in the dictatorships from the states' determination to monopolize industry—a more rigid control over profits meant that the golden days of 1914–18 were no more. And besides, victory for France would mean in all probability merely a prolongation of some form of the People's Front while victory for Germany would bring an extension of Herr Hitler's almost magical way of controlling unruly labor and of neutralizing the aspirations of the masses. Had the war been against Russia, of course, the story might have been different and, indeed, the winter of 1940 gave curious evidence of their hysteria in this regard.

This was the fatal last winter of freedom for France. Poland was defeated, Belgium and Holland uneasily neutral; Italy, Russia and Japan were coldly threatening; and Germany was massing her implacable might for the kill. Only England and France were opposing this mountain of distrust, hostility and fear. Attack was impossible. Furthermore the long hesitancies of Blum and Daladier which had resulted in a reluctant neutrality toward Spain had meant that France must now protect still a third border. A neutrality so ungracious had produced no friendship from Spain, and it seemed necessary, as it was, to retain thousands of troops as guards along this mountainous border stretch separating France from Italy and Spain. These troops were thus immobilized for the greater part of the war, and their lack upon the battlefields when the crisis came was one of the many dreary factors of defeat.

But while these troops idled fearfully, while the entire General Staff stood around helplessly, realizing their utter inability to attack and wondering with increasing apprehension just what would be France's fate in the event of a blitzkrieg such as annihilated Poland, the entire fascist press was screaming with woe and indignation over the fate of Finland, demanding, moreover, that France, which could by no means now control her own fate, should rush to the rescue of this pitiful victim of the hated Russians! Those who had clamored that

Frenchmen should not die for Danzig were now demanding that all of France should die, if need be, for Helsinki. Two hundred million enemies more or less, ringing every border, held no terrors or shocks for these friends of Otto Abetz, but the cruel fate of Finland wrung every fascist heart and aroused an indignation that the fate of France herself had never been able to produce among the enemies of the Republic.

Actually the plan for war against Russia made headway in spite of the realities at home. And, incredible as it now sounds against the perspective of the more recent past, General Weygand succeeded in having placed under his command an army of several hundred thousand with whom he was preparing to attempt the conquest of the Caucasus from Syria.

In the light of actual Russian achievement, of the successive failure of what had been generally considered the world's mightiest army to make any material headway against the solid might of Soviet force, the appalling ineptitude of French military thinking at this time may be estimated. Against the impregnable chain of the Caucasus, against equipment which has measured itself against that of the German *Wehrmacht* and proved its superiority, General Weygand was solemnly preparing to hurl half a million Frenchmen, on foot, on camels or on horses; armed with rifles, revolvers, bayonets and a few machine guns; possessing no tanks and almost no artillery.

The war in France was over almost before it started—long before this unhappy army of Weygand could begin its suicidal mission. But as soldiers and potential defenders against the enemy at home, they too were immobilized, stranded far from the place where the need was greatest and completely idle, while the lack of a few supplementary divisions at Sedan set in motion the most appalling military disaster in the long history of France.

But this scheme was to fascinate the French admirers of Hitler and his New Order almost up to the fatal day in June which saw the end of the Third Republic. Their arguments were simple and repetitious. They were not deluded by the Russo-German pact and in this respect at least they showed discernment. They reasoned that, at heart, Hitler still despised Russia and the Communists and was merely waiting his own good time to engulf them. Furthermore, was he not demonstrating his benevolence toward France by so considerately refraining from engaging her idle armies? And so an attack upon Russia by France would indicate to Hitler the sympathy of a nominal enemy and would hasten the day when, Hitler having finished what France had started, the French who were on the right side could conclude their peace with the New Order, secure in its protection and possessing a government purged once and for all of the successive chills and fevers of democracy. Even Frenchmen less deluded by the New Order myth fell partly into this trap, except that in their hearts they dreamed of a Germany which would be exhausted by its battle with Russia and therefore ready to conclude peace with France and leave the country to go its own chosen and accustomed way.

Brooding in his handsome embassy at Burgos, the Marshal weighed chances and possibilities. He was not entirely happy about the situation, but at the same time he saw many comforting features. As 1940 dawned Hitler had not yet attacked. It was always possible that the indefatigable appeasers, Daladier and Chamberlain, were working out some form or other of negotiated peace that would buy off the rapacious Germans for another breathing spell. Should that happen, the prestige of having ended a difficult situation with no worse loss would go to Daladier, and the Marshal would once more have been sidetracked.

But as Pétain plotted and debated with the Spanish friends to whom he so confidently predicted an uprising in France, Hitler acted. The attack began upon May 9 and the Marshal knew that the hour had come.

The French Army, poorer by the 1,200,000 men stationed along the Italian border, the double Spanish border of Morocco and the Pyrenees and in Syria, bore the brunt of a terrible onslaught. And now Pétain began to feel that he could not lose. Either the French Army would hold the enemy at bay, thus proving once and for all time the conclusive superiority of a planned defense, or the army would fall back slowly and the Marshal would be called to take complete control.

But the slow setbacks quickly became a shameful and appalling rout. Daladier and Gamelin were the first scapegoats. Weygand was recalled from Syria without having had time to launch his fantastic Caucasian attack and, far from being rebuked for having undertaken so great a diversion at so crucial a moment, was given supreme command. And the Marshal, his old heart divided between chagrin at seeing his defensive divisions swept around like sawdust by the implacable onslaught of the panzer divisions and a discreet satisfaction at seeing a faster approach of the day when he might at last realize his ambition, returned to Paris. He came back in triumph, at the request of the tragic little scapegoat of a generation of mistakes and wrong guesses, Paul Reynaud. Under Reynaud, the Marshal became Minister of National Defense and Vice Premier. And bewildered, unhappy France took a little heart again.

CHAPTER 7

THE GREAT CONFIDENCE TRICK

TO THE FRENCHMAN in the street the name of Weygand evoked compelling memories of Foch. Weygand had been the generalissimo's chief of staff, an obedient and dutiful officer, executing the complicated strategical plans conceived by Foch with competence and dispatch. Weygand was often described as "another Foch." Gamelin's role in relation to Joffre had been the same as that of Weygand to Foch, but unhappily it had taken all too short a time for Gamelin to prove that he was not another Joffre. Had Joffre decided to defend a Maginot Line, had he decided to await battle there, no power on earth would have dislodged the sturdy old peasant until his professional conscience told him the time had come to move.

Weygand throughout his entire career had carried out the orders of his superiors. He had done this conscientiously, but as a generalissimo he had one overwhelming drawback. He had never commanded an army in the field. Until 1940 his outstanding achievement had been to restore discipline in the disorganized Polish Army of 1920 and to lead it successfully in the campaign against Russia. At the time the Polish Army had practically disintegrated, owing to the inefficiency of its generals, and it was engaged in fighting what amounted to a rabble of Communists, inexperienced in warfare and fighting under untrained officers. Weygand had reorganized the Poles and replanned their campaign, turning an incipient rout into victory. Actually it was a competent but by no means a miraculous military performance; but viewed from a distance, it took on the aura of a miracle to the sorely troubled French. Weygand, who had once saved Poland, was the man to save his own unhappy country.

But when Weygand found himself facing the magnificent German organization his essential lack of initiative and experience became apparent. The general who now was holding for the first time the field command of an entire army rapidly and tragically began to demonstrate his own utter inadequacy for the task in hand.

But the man who had chosen this dangerously inexperienced leader for the armies of France in her direst need was to the people generally a tower of strength. With Pétain as vice premier, the plain citizen of France relaxed in the thought that now the nation's fate was in the best possible hands.

This plain citizen did not realize how subtle a betrayer is age. Pétain had, it is true, been a good, though not a great, Frenchman, if by "great" is meant the qualities of soul and mind which make for greatness as distinct merely from fame. He had, within the limited sphere in which he had chosen to specialize, been a great general. But as the years had done their eroding work, this Frenchman had become by slow degrees a fascist; and the capacities of a once great general had stood still, frozen in the outmoded mold of the defensive concept of war. The military destiny of France was wholly within the hands of an old, obstinate and uncomprehending politico-militarist, and a subordinate to whom the word of superior authority remained law, no matter how inadequate or even dangerously in error that authority might be.

General Weygand wanted victory at the start, as any officer would do. But, as the Marshal before him had been, he was at heart a defeatist. The once great army of France, now smaller and pitifully ill equipped to face the hazards of mechanized war, was faced with a hopeless task. Before that army had even been fully engaged in battle the hope of victory had been abandoned and the leaders were brooding instead upon the dangers of a revolution born of defeat—as though the victorious German Army were likely to permit much headway to the counter-movement of communism.

But so far the old Marshal's betrayals had been largely of the mind or matters of passive consent, such as lending his name in secret to countenance the schemes of bolder plotters. Only now did he take, with full deliberation, the step which made him a conscious deceiver of the French people, a plotter conniving at the defeat of the will of his countrymen, a man who, having weighed the issues, sided with the enemy against his native land. For, however he may have disguised this motive later, however often and laboriously he may have referred to the regeneration of France, the Marshal knew well what he did when he accepted from the sorely beset people the power of deciding life or death for their country.

When he took dictatorial powers from the crumbling Reynaud Cabinet, the French people were doubly deceived. They were giving this supreme trust to a largely legendary figure, the symbol of unbreakable resistance, the hero who, with his back to the walls of Verdun, had cried, "*Ils ne passeront pas!*" The man who actually received it from them was, as we have shown, far from a fighter to the death, and as far from the French patriot he had been at the time of Verdun. He was, furthermore, a man tacitly committed to a deal with the forces which now were crushing France, and committed in such a fashion that the terms of the deal would almost certainly be theirs, not his.

And so he took the power of a dictator over France, already pledged to recognize defeat, while to the people he stood as a symbol of resistance. And in another sense also they were deceived. For this old man who had played for so long with the idea of rescuing his country from democracy via the road of politico-military dictatorship had not until now really conceived of the ruthless might of a dictatorship determined to win its way by force. Secretly he was appalled at the ruin this modern army already had wrought in France and the Low Countries. His earlier dreams of a war of attrition, of a victory through defense, were thoroughly shattered now. His own dictatorship was still reasonably safe, for that had been part of the bargain. But he now began to see that the thoroughness of defeat must mean that he would be not the equal in power and prestige of Hitler, Mussolini and Franco, but largely their creature, dependent upon their protection for a continuance of power, responsible to them for the behavior of the grieved and outraged French people.

Fed for years upon the belief in his own magnificence, this did not immediately seem so overwhelming a tragedy to the Marshal. True, he could not now halt the war without overwhelming sorrow and defeat for France, a defeat which leaders of his choice, acting upon his own ideas, were making more tragically inevitable day by day. But it would, he felt sure, be quite simple for him to negotiate with Hitler, who admired him so, a peace which would preserve for the sensitive French their national dignity and honor, and enable him to set about the sweeping reforms in government that alone could remake the nation nearer to the vague and imitative heart's desire of the old would-be autocrat.

At this period a miracle might still have saved France. But miracles are conditioned for the most part upon blind faith and a willingness to receive inspiration. Neither of these conditions applied to France's leaders. Both Marshal Pétain and General Weygand had accepted the inevitability of defeat. The unconquerable faith of a Churchill was utterly beyond them. A miracle was out of the question for the uninspired, bewildered and discouraged armies which waited for the word of hope and courage that never came.

In 1914, after the disaster of Charleroi, the *poilus* fled on foot to the Marne. Weighed down with their heavy equipment, hampered by a complete lack of modern motorized assistance, in eight days of stifling midsummer heat they managed to cover three hundred kilometers, bringing after them into a trap the prematurely rejoicing enemy. Once the Germans had been separated from their supporting artillery, the fleeing French turned and tackled them and, under Joffre, won the victory of the Marne. But no such generalship, no such single-minded devotion inspired the armies of 1940. Officers and men were united neither in conviction nor in devotion. The poison of years of political chicanery and of ceaseless enemy propaganda now was doing its fatal work. One group was lukewarm about defeating Germany because it sympathized vaguely with Nazism. Another group, still not understanding clearly why the second great war of a generation had come about, felt itself united in sympathy with the German people, against these mysterious men who always seemed able to bring about war. Still others, while hating Nazism, nevertheless regarded it as the only bulwark in Europe against Marxist communism. And still other smaller factions were anti-Semitic or anticlerical. It was an army divided by its separate fears and not united upon the one common point, a hope and confidence in victory.

A unity which has been destroyed through years of a doubtful peace cannot be rebuilt in a hurry when war at last strikes. There was no time now for Frenchmen to learn understanding and a common resolve. The men, divided from their officers by social as well as ideological cleavages, had no time to become inured to the hardships of this new type of warfare. It might perhaps have been possible for a ruthless and selfless patriot to restore order and confidence, but it would have been at the cost of a terrible overhauling, the execution of hundreds of traitors in high places, the granting to men of resolution the authority to take drastic action upon their own responsibility. The cost would have been great and the result problematical. But nobody was at hand to try it.

One of the fatal errors was the decision to retreat across the flat plains of southwestern France instead of into the rocky and difficult countryside of Brittany. The vast tracts of the Loire Valley offered a superb opportunity to the ceaselessly moving panzer divisions of the enemy. Here the French soldier moved only to be cut down or captured in the Germans' good time. A less propitious place for battle with an armored invader could not have been chosen. But had the war been carried by France to Brittany, had the enemy had to try his luck in that rocky and difficult country, the story might still have been different. This peninsula jutting out to sea, separated by only a few miles of Channel from England, could have been reinforced indefinitely by the British. And, had evacuation still become necessary, a million soldiers might have left the ports of the Breton coast for England, to fight again another day. Instead they left weapons and hope behind as they trudged off to the concentration camps of the enemy.

But both Weygand and Pétain were convinced, early in the battle, that the war was lost. Now Pétain's single aim, and therefore Weygand's, was to conclude it as soon as possible and on terms acceptable to Germany. And to understand this incredible viewpoint and all that it involved, it is necessary to go back again for a few years in the life of the Marshal.

In 1935 he had attended, with other European dignitaries, the funeral of Marshal Pilsudski of Poland. Here the vain and credulous old man was the especial object of the flatteries of Air Marshal Goering. Repeatedly the corpulent and tactful Goering assured the old man of the extravagant esteem in which he was held by the leaders of the Reich. Alone among Frenchmen, he declared, Marshal Pétain possessed the full sympathy and admiration of the Fuehrer. He alone had seen the traps and dangers of communism concealed in the specious freedoms of democracy. The leading dictator of Europe felt a strong spiritual communion between himself and France's ancient hero.

The wily Goering embroidered his theme in a manner certain to command the Marshal's close attention. Herr Hitler, he announced, had made his own analysis of the battles of the Great War and of the defeat of sections of the German Army. It was his conviction, so his aide and confidant assured Pétain, that the honors of that war were unfairly bestowed; that France's real hero and greatest soldier was not Foch but Pétain.

The Marshal turned thirsty ears to such unsubtle flatteries. What a pity that such intelligent men might someday find themselves involved in war with France! Goering followed up his advantage, first with compliments to France's "magnificent army" and then with a hint that, if war ever should mar the harmony between the two countries, with France emerging the victor, he and Hitler might find the anguish of yielding somewhat mitigated if the noble and impartial Pétain were their conqueror. And with this grandiose assurance went an implied suggestion that if the fortunes of war should reverse this eventuality the Marshal might find them as amiable and benignant victors as they expected to find him.

This exchange lay dormant a long time in the mind of the Marshal, and until recently it had not occurred to him that the second suggestion might ever become a possibility. But now, with the naked might of his friends revealing itself with new terrors almost daily, this five-year-old conversation returned more frequently to mind. He alone, apparently, could win for his country the peace with honor customary among gentleman soldiers. He alone could rescue France at the eleventh hour from the consequences of too long an indulgence in democracy, and his rewards would be the gratitude and obedience of an awakened French people and the friendship and understanding of Europe's powerful men. To the heavy laurels of the unvanquished old soldier and hero would be added a new crown. He would become the political savior of the nation, having once before saved it in war. Once the peace was achieved, the frenzied adoration of all of France, not of the restless and discontented few, would at last be his.

But first it would be necessary to convince France that further struggle against her hereditary enemy was useless, that her armies were outmatched. This was not easy. Beside it the task of persuading a humiliated and beaten nation that her salvation lay in an old man she trusted and had honored would be simple.

For the first exercise in persuasion, Pétain had recourse to powerful allies. By now, having seen the probable end in sight, the opportunists of all parties were beginning to jockey for influence under the new dispensation. A Laval, a Caillaux, had no scruples about making themselves comfortable in a government approved by the conquerors. The same was true of Déat, Marquet, De Brinon and so on. It was perhaps a little more surprising to find Chautemps in this company. This former president of the Radicals, the defender of Stavisky, for whom he had ruined his party, now became suddenly the ardent admirer of the Rightists' hero, Marshal Pétain.

But the two were not so dissimilar in spirit after all. In that last tragic meeting of the Cabinet it was Chautemps who succeeded in persuading two ministers to change their minds, so that a slim majority vote of thirteen to eleven was cast in favor of seeking an armistice. Then Reynaud resigned, to be succeeded by Pétain as dictator. For this service M. Chautemps reaped the rich reward he had come to expect of his trades and compromises. He left France as all of her tragedies came upon her and lived for months in Washington, as the Marshal's personal representative, at the not unhandsome salary (for the unaccredited representative of the leader of a defeated nation) of $2,000 a month. His presence and his activities finally enraged even the amenable Henry-Haye, the Marshal's official ambassador to the United States, and at last the salary being paid by a France bled white by her conquerors was discontinued.

By his final step the Marshal achieved his longing and retained intact the prestige of an undefeated general. Upon his aide and scapegoat, General Weygand, fell all the crushing ignominy of defeat, although that defeat had been prepared for years past by the egotism and blindness of the now triumphant chief.

For there can be no question that the Marshal, in tone and attitude, regarded himself as a victor. To the beaten people upon whom he tirelessly urged the virtues of humility and self-denial he spoke in the vainglorious tones of a conqueror. And in thus encouraging this self-deception lay one of Hitler's greatest psychological triumphs. For it was the essence of his long campaign of flattery to persuade the Marshal that he could be the victorious leader of a defeated nation. All negotiations, all correspondence between them, at least in the honeymoon period of this tragic shotgun marriage, was conducted in these ceremonious forms. While systematic plans for the looting of beaten France were being put into swift effect, the exchange of courtesies between Hitler and his ancient puppet had a ring of oriental hyperbole.

But the Marshal alone was not equal to the labyrinths of political intrigue and complication now opening up before him. As a fitting cicerone for the new journey he chose with grisly appropriateness the vulturelike Pierre Laval, Germany's long-time broker in France. Caillaux, it is true, had similar claims to preference, but Laval was the cleverer of the two. Caillaux had a record of enmities within his own party that Laval had never risked. Caillaux was thought to be arrogant, whereas Laval's stock in trade was an unfailing, greasy good nature. Furthermore Laval had discovered a long time before the means of making himself indispensable to the Marshal. Having discovered the old man's still vigorous ambition, Laval had discreetly put him in touch with the fascist groups so assiduously organizing themselves in 1933, which later were to achieve a form of uneasy unity under the respectable front afforded by Pétain.

There was another reason why Laval was considered of value in 1940. He still boasted of his friendship with Mussolini, had never entirely relinquished hope of the "Latin bloc" which would have united the Catholic authoritarian regimes of Europe in a group excluding the so-called democracies, presented a solid front to "Godless Russia" and maintained a relationship of wary amiability with the newer, Aryan dictatorships typified by Germany. Curiously enough, France, which had retained until too late her illusions as to the lack of menace presented by German expansion, retained a lively suspicion and fear of the Italian corporate state. France's appeasers foresaw no trouble in working out an amicable armistice with Germany but felt that Italy's last-minute stab presaged violent and humiliating territorial demands. And in this event Pierre Laval with his valuable friendships would, it was felt, be a useful man to have around.

And indeed he soon proved invaluable to the new regime. With the assistance of Chautemps, of Caillaux and Malvy, two traitors of an earlier day, he even found it simple to persuade the French Parliament to sign its own death warrant. Although, under the circumstances now developing, few parliamentarians wished to continue with the responsibilities of government or to sign their names to the type of armistice or peace treaty imminently in prospect. And so it was not difficult to persuade a majority to sign away "provisionally" their governing authority in order to evade responsibility for the dirty work. The shrewder among them were already laying plans for a resumption of their careers once the old man who now was seizing the reins should resign or die. It had not then occurred to them that once their authority was relinquished it would be impossible, without wholesale armed revolt, to take it back again.

Now the Marshal, for a brief while, was happy. He had joined that exalted company of European dictators, Hitler, Mussolini, his friend Franco, Horthy and Salazar. And he was now empowered, still shining with his new glory, to tackle the armistice negotiations which were to restore France to a peaceful and respected status.

This period of self-congratulation did not last long. The Marshal now was finding himself in an appalling dilemma, and one from which he could not emerge without sacrificing either his own ambitions or the honor of France. Repeatedly he had announced that he would conclude only a peace with honor. This would have been difficult if not impossible to achieve in all sincerity, since France's pledge to England made the signing of a separate armistice an act impossible to reconcile with honor. Propaganda had, of course, worked hard upon this point, insisting that England herself was probably seeking a way out of the war and that in this dire emergency France must first consider her own needs.

But these specious arguments could not really have deceived the Marshal, who in his time had clung to exalted ideas of the chivalry proper among honorable enemies. He had managed to convince himself (on the thinnest of evidence, it is true) that his personal prestige would win for France terms not incompatible with the national honor. But to his consternation terms of incredible harshness were imposed with the most flattering personal courtesy. He could not withstand the courtesy although his soul realized clearly enough the price France was asked to pay for the countenancing of his dictatorship.

But his most grievous fault as a negotiator, and one which makes it almost wholly impossible to believe that any good faith was inherent in his action, was that he announced to the French people that he was suing for an armistice before any negotiation had even been agreed upon. By this broadcast, delivered in his rôle as dictator, he at one stroke destroyed any bargaining power he may have had and broke the back of French military and civilian resistance. He accompanied his announcement, furthermore, by a cease-firing order, given before his proposal could possibly have been accepted.

The results were immediate and appalling. During the brief period of negotiations the French Army lost more than one million men as prisoners, twice as many as during the entire rest of the war, including the blitzkrieg, had cost. Men who might have sacrificed their lives to make possible at least a semblance of victory saw no object in continued fighting when even the head of the state had announced that it was no longer of any use.

Every day that passed added to the demoralization and the disaster. The Marshal now could measure the results of his actions and sense their effect upon the victors, who saw no need for extravagant concession once the end of fighting was actually announced to the beaten foe. Now it would have been difficult for him to retreat from his request even had he chosen to do so. He had denied the insistent requests of General de Gaulle that the army be permitted to retreat by way of Brittany. This would have meant that French troops could battle their way in thousands to Brest and Lorient, St. Brieux and St. Malo, well within the protective power of British planes and capable of evacuating almost an entire army. Instead it had been he who ordered the southward retreat of the army toward Bordeaux and Marseille, where plane protection was thin and impossible to strengthen and where the disheartened soldiers were almost completely at the mercy of German bombers. It had seemed, when this decision was taken, merely an extra means of insuring that the war could not be prolonged indefinitely. But then the prospects of a friendly and generous peace also had seemed more cheerful. Now, as the harsh terms were made known with inflexible politeness, it was impossible to retrieve the rout in the south and to make continued fighting an alternative to more favorable terms. The enemy could make his own terms, and he did.

There was, however, still the possibility of flight for the government. Holland, Belgium and Norway had set the example, and France was still master of a vast empire and a powerful fleet. But this last possible trick was forestalled. When the emissaries of the Marshal suggested that the war might still be continued from afar if more favorable terms were not forthcoming, the answer was sharp and decisive: if the Pétain government did not wish to accept, Germany would simply install another government, ready and waiting under the leadership of Mm. Doriot and Déat, which would sign with no further quibbling. One way or another, Germany would obtain the terms she sought.

Thus the Marshal's last flicker of doubt and dismay over the course he had chosen to pursue died down. Confronted with this choice—unconditional surrender to all the terms imposed or relinquishment of the passionately cherished goal now so nearly within his grasp—ambition won. France was sold to her enemy.

The Marshal sold his country for a tinsel crown. He had succeeded in obtaining the power to reign over France, in a Europe now dedicated to the Hitlerian New Order and awaiting only the imminent fall of England to become resigned to an indefinite night of slavery. The Marshal had not the shadow of a belief in the possibility of British resistance. If France could not survive for more than five weeks, who could do better? To refuse to sign the armistice because England was still fighting would have been a gesture of which the Marshal of World War I days might have been proud. Now it seemed merely an idle quixotry, to sacrifice the possibility of being one of the chiefs of the new Europe for the sake of a few more weeks of British resistance.

No, he could not sacrifice France to vermin like Déat and Doriot. France needed him and he would stay; the country would be grateful that he, in person, would be their intermediary with the victors.

CHAPTER 8

THE CROSSROADS OF BETRAYAL

WHEN THE OUTRAGED and bewildered French people, upon whom the gates of the prison were already closing, tried to grasp the terms of the armistice agreed to by their leader, they sought in their numbness to find a few crumbs of comfort in the debacle. Individually the people prized liberty as much as Frenchmen ever did. Collectively they were disheartened by the twenty-year history of political ineptitude and corruption which, with the exception of a few bright phases, had tarnished the name of the Third Republic.

Their attitude, one of the causes of their downfall, has been soundly explained by Raoul de Roussy de Sales, who said, in *The Making of Tomorrow*: "Many people today are inclined to think that Aristotle is right and that democracy does inevitably lead to tyranny. But this can happen only when the institutions have become so weak or so discredited that they lose all authority. The desire for authority then becomes so great—especially in times of crisis—that it will inevitably be transferred to one man. This man is called Marshal Pétain in France today, Hitler in Germany. They may appear to be very different but the process that has brought them to power is the same: the Third Republic had ceased to operate and the Weimar Republic never had operated."

French demoralization at this point was final and complete.

Weary, stunned with shock, few of them could think of any good reason why they should resist to the death simply to restore a patched-up Chautemps Cabinet to all the perquisites of office. But at least out of this crushing disaster they now had the Marshal, too venerable for worldly ambition, too honest to betray them, a man who already saw himself as the wise and kindly father of a sorely troubled people.

Even the inclusion of the wily Laval in the new government did not at this moment disconcert the people. Laval had shown himself a clever and cunning negotiator. He was, moreover, a good friend of the Nazis and fascists and in this bleak new world one must take one's friends as one found them. He could perhaps obtain a better bargain than other less compromising Frenchmen would dare ask.

The people did not know how completely all bargaining power had passed from the hands of the conquered to those of the conquerors. Negotiation now had resolved itself simply into a matter of submitting or quitting; into accepting a take-it-or-leave-it proposition or making way for a more accommodating regime.

The Marshal had reached the very crossroads of betrayal. He had not suddenly found himself there with no idea of the road he had traveled. That road had been very long and devious and there had been many opportunities for a swift return to the highway had he been so minded. Even now it was not too late. Life had little left to offer so old a man and the chance of sacrificing his life if need be to inspire in the leaderless French people one last magnificent flare of resistance was his to take. There is little doubt but that the people would have responded, whatever the cost.

But the choice was an intolerable one for the Marshal. It was not alone that he had so easily persuaded himself that if he yielded now to an insane impulse France would find herself in the hands of much worse men. There was also the consideration that in so renouncing the deal he had almost consummated he would thereby be placing himself in the wrong, admitting to many and serious mistakes, perhaps even offering himself up for judgment and condemnation by the future rulers of France. This thought was intolerable.

One of the paramount aspects of the Marshal's psychological make-up must always be remembered in evaluating his actions at this stage. He is one of the most convincedly self-righteous of men. There is no record of his ever having admitted a mistake or acknowledged a poor judgment. He began life with the rigid obstinacy of mind which alone can make such humorless blindness credible. And throughout a long lifetime in the natural authoritarianism of army life, crowned with a twenty-five-year term as virtual dictator of the army, this conviction of rightness and righteousness had grown into an obsession. Wherever events clearly placed him in the wrong, it was the events which were wrong and not he. Therefore an explanation of the actions which had ended so grievously, the possible need of self-justification before critical people, appeared to him not a tragic though inevitable consequence of mistake, but an intolerable affront to which under no circumstances he should justly be subjected.

Actually there now stood on record against him at least five major mistakes.

First, he had persisted in believing that it would be simple, with the aid of the static magic of the Maginot Line, to beat whatever Germany had to offer. Indeed his major worry for some years had been not the ceaseless and inventive preparation on the other side of the Rhine but the thought that the German Army might prove too easy a victim to the outmoded and ill-equipped French forces, thus affording no clear-cut and triumphant test of his theories of defensive war. All his influence in 1936, '37 and '38 had been cast against a war with Germany which might then have been easily won. He had veered sharply and drastically only in 1939 when the German might was reinforced by spoils from Czechoslovakia and had acquired also the tremendous material and psychological advantages of the pact with Russia.

Secondly, he followed up years of unthinking optimism with an equally unreasoning defeatism when the blitz was launched. Once the well-timed blows had struck France to her knees he was instantly convinced that she would never rise again and that the enemy was invincible.

Thirdly, all of his ancient Anglophobia arose at this stage to confirm his conviction that the British would never remain in the war once the incredible fact of French defeat became apparent. He used this argument at Bordeaux in order to influence still reluctant ministers to proceed with negotiations for the separate peace. The British Empire, he insisted, would soon ask for an armistice itself, and would perhaps even begin her bargaining before France. Thus she, and not the French, might seize the advantage. Why should not France for once be the more astute and obtain for herself a most-favored-nation treatment in defeat? These arguments powerfully influenced the vacillators, who were further swayed by the prophecy, frequently heard from General Weygand in those days, that any show of belligerence from Churchill would mean that England's neck would be "wrung like a chicken's" within the space of a few weeks. A year later Churchill himself was able to add to this the facetious comment, "Some chicken, some neck."

Fourthly, the Marshal concluded that Russia would be a

pushover for German military might—a mistake in which he was certainly not alone and which was dictated by the same type of wishful thinking animating other believers in the theory that nothing could be worse than communism.

Fifthly, he was convinced of the permanence of American neutrality. Even if by some miracle this could be abridged, any help from this source would almost certainly be reluctant and therefore both too little and too late.

In addition Marshal Pétain fantastically overestimated both his own value in the eyes of France and his influence as the master of her destiny. He had his own pessimistic ideas upon that destiny and had no doubt of the correctness and the popularity of his vision of France, happy in defeat, restored to the simplicities of an agricultural civilization, mystically resigned to expiate its sins in the pursuit of "Travail, Famille, Patrie." Freedom in such a picture was a negligible factor. There would be no need for freedom in a land where every family toiled upon its land, resigned in the faith that its wise parent decided every question and made no errors.

Furthermore the myth of German invincibility, now spread as assiduously as, a few years before, the myth of its impossibility had been, was an excellent counterblow to the failure of defense as exemplified in the tragically futile monument of the Maginot Line. Obviously if an opponent is invincible, then no strategy can avail against him and no stigma can attach to those who opposed him inadequately.

To this easy defense the British resistance provided a crushing reply. Obviously Germany was not invincible if, across a short space of water a foe obviously unprepared, inadequately armed, much smaller in size and lacking in a military tradition, could continue in its defiance for month after month, meanwhile building up from scratch an air force equal even to the Luftwaffe and dispersing piece by piece hastily assembled armies to battlefronts thousands of miles apart.

As the British proved that their determination was no mere gallant gesture one might have expected that the Marshal, given one last chance at retrieving his own and his country's honor, would have rejoiced that an ally he had abandoned had managed thus to save herself. He might now have begun to consider the possibilities of French resistance revitalized from the colonies and lending its helping hand to the slowly reviving British. But this would have been entirely contrary to the mind which had emerged from a lifetime of belief in its own infallibility. Simply by proving him wrong the British excited in the Marshal still more irritation and dislike. Already he had announced that the war was ended, that Germany was supreme, that it was useless for any power or combination of powers to stand against her. And here a power even less prepared than France was proving the prematureness of his conviction. Now, from being a conceivably unwilling victim of the conqueror, he must become, in order to uphold his own rightness, an active champion of the Nazi cause against that for which England still fights; that for which, until yesterday, France too was fighting.

Now the utterances which had been mournful justifications of France's unhappy fate became more and more the peevish denunciations of Germany's enemies. And those Frenchmen who had refused to bow to this frequently proclaimed inevitability became, not the heroes they are, but enemies and outcasts from their homeland. "He who is not with me is against me" never applied with greater truth than to Pétain, and he turned the sentiment, with steadily increasing indignation, against even those who fought for France on foreign soil and who deserved the tacit if not the overt encouragement of every man who still took pride in the name and the history of France.

Thus Pétain's anger and resentment against General de Gaulle, the promptness with which he added fresh names to the long list of those he has now declared traitors and deserters, was no comedy for German deception as millions of Frenchmen had pathetically hoped during the long months which followed the armistice. The steady condemnation of men whose only fault was that they insisted upon fighting for France, the arrest of long lists of their sympathizers, the handing over of hostages to the Germans—these at last drove home to increasing numbers of despairing Frenchmen the conviction that, abominable as it seemed, Marshal Pétain did not even wish for the delivery of France from her bondage.

During this fateful summer of 1940 and the autumn which followed, the whole world awaited with Pétain and his henchmen the fall of Great Britain and the dismemberment of her empire. Certainly it seemed inevitable, even to the devoted and agonizing friends of the British. The little island kingdom had no army to speak of; its navy, although still great, was grievously lacking in the corollary air arm necessary to protect the proud ships in the hazards of modern war. What she had had of modern equipment was either rusting on the sands of Dunkirk beach or was already in the service of the enemy. To resist invasion she had only a quietly imperturbable courage, a leader who embodied in his voice and person the very spirit of England. She had also, without knowing it at the time, a third great imponderable aid.

This was the incapacity for improvisation which was the one major weakness of the German General Staff. England has this, plus the incomparable valor of the people themselves, to thank for the fact that to this day she has remained proudly unconquerable.

This weakness that saved the world, this grain of sand that jammed and rendered helpless the entire complex machinery of German might during the days of its greatest opportunity, will make for historians of the future an endless and fascinating study. In its essentials it comes down to the simple fact that the meticulous attention to detail which heretofore had made the success of the German armies, in this instance turned to the benefit of Germany's enemy and against the boasted speed and drive of the mighty Reichswehr armies themselves.

Briefly, Nazi planning had foreseen the end of the Battle of France by the end of the summer of 1940 and with it the immediate plea for peace of the dangerously weakened lone foe, England. All of Von Ribbentrop's reports had proved to the Fuehrer that this would be the logical ending of England's share in the war. The "nation of shopkeepers," of petty businessmen and cautious, Red-scared county families would run true to the pattern of worn-out empires and gladly capitulate in exchange for a place in the Nazi sun, a colonial empire which would remain intact. And if recalcitrant elements clustering around the belligerent Churchill should seem disposed to urge continued resistance, then a series of bombings unprecedented in intensity should constrain the mass of the people to demand peace at the threat of revolt. Thus accounts with the British would be settled swiftly and cheaply, and after its few months of rest and the imposition of order in Europe the German Army would be free for its major task, the complete and unannounced subjugation of Russia. The ideological menace of the Soviets would then be eliminated and the incalculable riches of Siberia and the Caucasus would be freed for development by German engineers and technicians. Germany thus would have become mistress of the world, with no more fighting necessary, since the only possible opposition to a nation in control of five hundred million inhabitants would come from a possible coalition of the underpopulated, still free British dominions and the unprepared, still neutrally inclined United States.

This plan was prepared à l'Allemande, that is, down to the last meticulous detail. Examples of this attention to detail already had been given to an astonished world. On the very day the German Army marched into Paris, the newspaper Paris-Soir continued publication without the slightest interruption but under the New Order. And just in case the presses had been destroyed, the Nazis had thoughtfully brought with them complete fonts of the identical type faces which were so distinctive a feature of the Paris-Soir. When the occupying troops paid for their purchases they did so with the special currency prepared for the polite looting of occupied countries and on which was printed the year of issuance—1937!

But, fortunately for our side, this talent for organization has compensating disadvantages. With every detail prepared, the machine is too finely organized to permit swift changes of plan in the event of unforeseen circumstances. The plan will work only when its opponents behave exactly as the Nazis foresaw they would behave. The whole complex mechanism stalls when confronted with the unexpected. It stalled at the Marne in 1914 and it stalled again in 1940 when the British people refused to yield or to crumble into disunity as the master plan required. The entire nation, unanimous behind the magnificent defiances of Winston Churchill, refused to recognize defeat when it stared them in the face, and defeat, therefore, retreated in confusion.

Furthermore France had succumbed in June, three whole months before the peace offensive against Great Britain was due to start. The campaign that started, therefore, was weak and indecisive and made no impression whatever upon the British people. And it was impossible for the General Staff to swing around its gigantic war machine in time against the unprotected coasts of England. Thus three irreplaceable months were lost. In those three months the British were stiffened in courage, the gallant few of the Royal Air Force showed how incredibly much they could do against many, and the zero hour for Great Britain was past, never to return. For the great momentum was under way, and its reversal was impossible on so short a notice. It was Russia, not Great Britain, that Germany was committed to attack.

Now the German General Staff had something of the idea of Pétain and his collaborationist assistants on this turn of affairs. Somebody was cheating. It was not on the cards that the British should resist, that this idiotic assemblage of youths in old planes and soldiers without guns should be seriously prepared to oppose themselves to the might of German arms. By doing so when defeat was so obviously inevitable they were simply prolonging the discomforts of war, postponing the day when the New Order should be solidified throughout Europe for the benefits of Greater Deutschland. And from the viewpoint of the new Vichy government this ignorant resistance was having serious consequences. Certainly the armistice pledge to Germany of indemnity payments of four hundred million francs daily was not made in the expectation of a long-drawn-out war. All of the cowardly compromise implicit in the Vichy agreements was based upon the swift collapse of England, the quick ending of the war and the signing of a peace treaty which would give to France the position of favorite vassal of the master state.

The true extent of the rage and general frustration of the German High Command is only now beginnnig to be seen in its true perspective. Their power was such that even if the invasion had cost them a hundred thousand men they would still have been able to land on the British coast a formidable armored force which would have met only a shapeless aggregation of half-trained soldiers, elderly men with rifles and staves and with no support of tanks, howitzers, field guns or the newer weapons of war. The power of the British fleet under such circumstances would necessarily have been limited, opposed as it must have been by attack from land-based bombers, torpedo planes and the tremendous force of land barrages from the French coast.

And yet Germany could not undertake this tempting, this simple venture! And the reason was that all of her preparations were being directed toward Russia and not toward England. There simply was not sufficient mobility in the plans and the planning minds to reverse all of this ponderous preparation so as to take advantage of opportunity and to subdue by force what could not be taken by alternate threat and promise. They tried still other means of achieving a bought peace rather than the one they could have imposed by force. Since the British were too proud to sue for it, Hitler even graciously indicated his willingness to take them into partnership upon his Russian venture if they would only cease opposition. This was the explanation of the Hess mission, undertaken as a last-minute gesture of magnanimity. How completely it backfired, becoming, instead of a German weapon, a new tonic for the already flourishing morale of the British, the world now knows. And this move too was based upon the complete misunderstanding of the British mind achieved by Von Ribbentrop upon the basis of his acquaintance with a few elderly appeasement-minded peers and their hysterical offspring. Because Churchill, like his predecessors Chamberlain and Baldwin, had been outspoken in his dislike of the Soviet government's aims and achievements, Hitler, advised by his salesman-ambassador, was convinced that the help of so powerful an ally as Germany in the subjugation of this menace would be welcome enough to cancel out all subsidiary differences and past hostilities.

And so the Hess mission turned into a British triumph. Great Britain warned Russia of the impending attack which it was now too late for Germany to countermand, notwithstanding the utter confusion of circumstances which now surrounded it, and a new coalition of power was originated for the salvation of the civilized world.

If British obduracy was a surprise and an annoyance for Hitler, to Pétain it seemed an insult. He, the supreme strategist, again was being proved wrong. His decision that the war was lost was, as it had been twenty-five years before, being contested and overruled by British arrogance. And France, which had signed a temporary armistice looking toward a favorable, permanent peace, now seemed likely to be saddled for months, perhaps years, with a hateful, ruinous partition, an army of uniformed locusts which with quiet voracity were eating away the life and the wealth of France, and a tireless overseership which day by day stretched more thinly the veil of polite deference masking its ceaseless pressures and demands.

Pétain had proclaimed the need of defeat for corrupt democracy. His mind had been decided long before war began, and the ruthless efficiency of totalitarian might had merely confirmed his judgment. He had stopped the fighting to spare the sinful people of France from further slaughter and to enable them to expiate in poverty and labor the crimes of the Third Republic. But the British, given the same opportunity, had chosen to spurn it.

Against the English, having left them alone in their need, he now could do little. But the full fury of his resentment and dismay was saved for those Frenchmen who chose to disregard his plain orders and who fought their way, against all of the obstacles and punishments he with the Germans had been able to devise, to stand with England for the future deliverance of France. In order to justify the German victory, which he had decided was ordained, he turned even against those Frenchmen in whom the hope of France is now bound up. They, not the men who aided every German robbery of Frenchmen, incurred his angry denunciation. Their continued existence, the success which at long last begins to crown their efforts, are to him personal affronts. He accepted without a sigh the news of the arrest and execution of thousands of hostages whose only crime has been that they were suspected of sheltering a Frenchman who sought to fight for France. A rage and a vengefulness far in excess of any show of passion required by the enemy dictated his prompt condemnations of men such as Generals de Gaulle and Giraud, or even such equivocal side-changers as Admiral Darlan. It was with the approval of Marshal Pétain that General de Lattre de Tassigny was sentenced to ten years in prison for believing that the hour of liberation was at hand. Generals de Gaulle and Catroux were condemned to death, Giraud and Darlan both were deprived of citizenship, merely for fighting, far removed from any possible control by the Marshal, to insure that the

France which had made them all should again someday know a proud and free future.

Now the full measure of the fall of this one-time patriot from the heights of the days of Verdun begins to be apparent. In those days he was often obstinate, often mistaken. But he was always a Frenchman. In the long years since, the pride, the stubbornness, the greedy appetite for flattery have perverted judgment too fatally for any possible correction.

The new man who succeeded the old is best exemplified by the broadcasts he addressed to the French people in the two years since the armistice. His first speech following the armistice began in the manner of the old kings of France: "We, Philippe Pétain." In August 1941 he announced with a strengthening of this new mood of feeble arrogance: "In 1917 I put an end to mutiny. In 1940 I put an end to rout."

Only a man blind to all the essential significance of his actions could so describe the tragedy of the armistice. By a complete surrender of his entire army, by an abject capitulation, he claims to have stopped a rout. Thus a physician might be expected to claim credit for halting an epidemic when the last man in his village has died of it!

Another example of how far his tolerance of the invader exceeded any normal requirement of enforced courtesy from the vanquished to the conqueror may be found in this same speech. In it the Marshal refers to: "the collaboration offered by the Chancellor of the Reich, *in terms of which I appreciate the deference* . . ." And again in this same utterance is this revealing view of the manner in which he might be expected to receive the prospects of a German defeat and the return of democratic government to Europe:

"If France did not understand that she was condemned by

the impact of events to change her regime, then she would see open before her the abyss in which the Spain of 1936 just missed being swallowed, and from which she was saved only by faith, youth and sacrifice. . . ."

For the Marshal as he stood at this time, the cruel fall of France was a benediction in which the country was purged of the Third Republic. German defeat would revive the whole distasteful question of free government and, in an atmosphere in which malcontents would once more be shouting of *Liberté, Egalité, Fraternité,* the Marshal might even be brought to trial and judged of his errors and betrayals. The trials of Riom would be reversed and their instigator might find himself in the dock, facing some unanswerable accusations. At long last the Marshal himself would be asked to account for the appalling unpreparedness of the French Army, for the long session of stupid neglect and of intrigues with traitors which had made of the proud army he had inherited from Foch one which could collapse from within under pressure from without.

Whatever the kind and well-meaning friends of France may have thought, however distressed they may have been at the thought of so old a man with so brave a history turning traitor upon the very edge of the grave, the Marshal himself made it irrefutably obvious that he would do his best to prevent a victory for the United Nations, that to him the enemy of his country was not Hitler, the deferential leech who has bled France white, while showing every courtesy to the Marshal. By this time the enemy was whoever was working to deliver France, and who in doing so spoke disparagingly of the Marshal and his judgments. Between Roosevelt, Churchill, De Gaulle, who dared to speak aloud against the farce of Vichy and the pretensions of its dictator, and Hitler who always remembered to be polite to the Marshal however harshly he might deal with France, the old man had made his final choice and it was for Hitler.

Thus Henri Philippe Pétain, the model of a willing loser, became the eager friend of the conqueror, the bitter enemy of his erstwhile allies, and a leader who scrupled not to snatch personal victory from the ruins of his country's disaster, more at home in the camp of the conquerors than with his defeated people who still dreamed obstinately of liberty and of the past and future of a free France.

And so, when the American landing in North Africa symbolized for millions of still silent Frenchmen the day of a liberation growing nearer, the Marshal gave the order and repeated it, to fire upon the liberators who had become the enemies. Once again he had determined: *"Ils ne passeront pas."* But the brave phrase now was aimed against the friends of his country. It was no longer the Germans who should not pass, but the Americans and their allies with whom once he had fought in common.

CHAPTER 9

THE TWO BLACKMAILERS

ONE INEXPLICABLE FACTOR in the German subjugation of France has been Hitler's apparent magnanimity on the subject of the French fleet and colonies. In June 1940 defeated France was in no position to bargain. Rather than lose his newly acquired prestige, the Marshal abandoned one after the other every possible bargaining point. Alsace-Lorraine, two million prisoners, the arbitrary partitioning of France, payment of the terrible indemnity of four hundred million francs daily for an indefinite period—all of these were accepted. The Marshal did not oppose the wholesale removal to Germany of vital segments of French industry, thus rendering impossible any resumption of normal industrial life; nor did he object to the robbery by which the controlling shares in French business passed by a series of paper transactions into German hands. All of these indignities and others too numerous to mention he accepted in exchange for the recognition of his supreme personal authority of what remained of France.

How and why, then, was he able to save the fleet and empire for so long? The mystery is capable of explanation.

Pétain's total lack of opposition to all of the other demands made by Hitler, his willing anxiety to agree with the wishes of the Reichschancellor, make it extremely unlikely that upon these two points alone he maintained a successful obstinacy.

Had Hitler really insisted upon assuming control over the French colonial domain, Pétain would undoubtedly have given way. Already the old man had sacrificed far more at home than was involved in the empire. Likewise it is difficult to believe that the bargainer who had given away every means of resuming warfare upon land would suddenly have begun to haggle over the transfer of a now useless fleet.

It seems more likely that the Fuehrer did not do much insisting where the fleet was concerned. It is possible, by deduction, to reconstitute what may have been his alternative.

At this particular time all the German advisers were quite sure that it would not be difficult to persuade England to retire from the war without further fighting. This end was thought to be more likely of achievement by diplomatic means than through force. It would be more subtle, so the reasoning probably ran, to refrain from causing English public opinion any undue concern over too great a concentration of maritime power in German hands. If the people could feel that they might withdraw from land fighting with their great navy still intact and supreme, they might, it was felt, be less sensitive to the defeat implied. Moreover, should they seize Admiral Darlan's ships, the combined might of the German-French fleets would be a threat which British advocates of continued resistance would not hesitate to use as an instance of the danger of withdrawing at this stage of the war.

However, it was equally necessary to make certain that there would be no chance of the French fleet continuing in the war at the side of the British. In order to insure this immobilization it was necessary to obtain the full consent of Admiral Darlan to the armistice conditions. As late as June 17, 1940, the Admiral was proclaiming his intention of continuing in the war with his still unconquered squadrons. But

Darlan's weak point was his boundless ambition. Although it might not be cheap or easy to buy him out, it was not impossible.

Long before the armistice became inevitable, the Marshal had set about winning the Admiral over to his point of view. Actually it was now Pétain who became the middle-man between Darlan and the German interests. Through his friend Franco the Marshal was kept fully informed of German plans in regard to France and as early as May 1940 he had begun negotiations with the ambitious sailor from Gascony. He held out the bait of a government of soldiers which would restore order in strife-ridden France and at the same time obtain the best possible terms of peace from Hitler. But the heads of this government, he insinuated, must be men of unquestioned prestige, having the authority to speak for France and the standing necessary to meet Hitler on terms as nearly equal as possible. And, continued the tempter, there were not many such men left in France. The Admiral and the Marshal remained almost the only two unconquered warriors. The Marshal was an old man. Therefore, if all negotiations went well, what more natural than that the Admiral who had been a party to them should succeed in office the chief of state to whom he was helper and trustworthy heir? Thus the Marshal showed himself not above the ruses resorted to by miserly millionaires, anxious to receive the best of attention from their hovering beneficiaries. He was, after all, eighty-four years old. And so, on June 18 of the same year, Admiral Darlan succumbed to his persuasions.

Darlan himself is still an enigma. Did he also decide that the situation was hopeless and that the only course was to retrieve whatever seemed personally possible from the wreckage? Or did he, as some of his partisans have maintained, accept a role in the Pétain government in order to try to retain within his own still patriotic hands the control which, later, he was to hand over to the Allies? His fortuitous presence in Algiers in November 1942 and the promptness with which he veered to the Allied side have been thought by many of Vichy's apologists to have tipped the balance in his favor. But the most likely explanation, from what is known generally of the man and his career, is that he was determined to steer himself and his fleet with sufficient skill and discretion to insure that whatever happened both would finish the war upon the winning side. Furthermore this opportunism was fortified by a mild Anglophobia, latent for some years, during which the Admiral's jealousy of the British fleet received no particular irritation, but active and growing, once the war brought the subordination of his ships to those of the larger navy.

However, in spite of his lack of affection for the British, Darlan was never wholeheartedly in the camp of the enemy either. A variety of promises frequently repeated was necessary to keep him safely within line. One account of these, and also of the impression that Darlan's curious personality, at the same time bluff and devious, had made upon at least one high-ranking Nazi is contained in a memorandum addressed to Marshal Pétain by General de la Laurencie. This unfortunate man had followed Pétain with a single-minded devotion during most of his army career. He had been a faithful accomplice during the Cagoulard conspiracies, and after the armistice he had been named as Vichy's first "Ambassador to Paris," thus preceding the notorious Fernand de Brinon. The memorandum here quoted was published last December in the Fighting French newspapers *La Marseillaise* and *Pour La Victoire*. When these papers obtained it, the General, whose personal fidelity had proved a patriotic second to his love for France, had been arrested and sentenced to a concentration camp. His crime had been that he had publicly declared: "I wish for, and I still believe in, a British victory."

Here is a part of his confidential report on conversations with Otto Abetz:

The personality of Admiral Darlan was mentioned when the subject of an eventual successor to the Marshal was discussed.

"We are," said Abetz, "opposed to the idea of a civilian dauphin."

"As a successor to the Marshal, who is old, who often changes his mind, who is ill advised, who represents the history of the past, it is necessary on the day of his disappearance to have a victorious military leader. Now, at this hour, you have none who, during the defeat, was able to keep his prestige intact, except the leader of the French Navy, Admiral Darlan. During the whole war and since the armistice, the French fleet fought magnificently. This is the only branch of the French war machine which has not been beaten.

"I have spoken personally with Admiral Darlan, who makes an excellent impression.

"When the English have been defeated, Europe will need a formidable navy for her continued defense.

"The French Navy has great and admirable traditions. Why should it not become the nucleus around which a European Navy might be constructed, *and why should not Admiral Darlan become head of this European Navy?* Just as Goering, who has brought our aviation arm to its present tremendous status, may perhaps become the future head of all European air power. . . ."

Abetz knows how to flatter the head of the French Navy with a rather obvious cleverness, but the flattery to which he already had recourse when he spoke to Admiral Darlan, during the personal interview on December 13, 1940, did not pass unnoticed. Admiral Darlan had fallen for it, had become intoxicated by it.

The horizons open to his personal ambitions were so full of promise that he did not hesitate—although they bore the German earmark—to pursue them even at the risk of hurting French opinion in its most intimate, its most praiseworthy sentiments. . . .

Darlan had shown clearly that he had no wish to join De Gaulle as the champion of a lost cause. Now the acknowl-edged heir-apparent of the Marshal, he had reason to look confidently toward the day when he too would be supreme head of a vassal state. Thus Hitler need not exert a dispropor-tionate amount of effort to retain the fleet, and with it a con-tinued dominance over those parts of the French Empire which still regarded themselves as subordinate to the Admiral. It has been believed by the larger proportion of Anglo-American opinion that only long and difficult arguments be-tween Pétain and Hitler had preserved the French Navy and colonial empire against German occupancy. The Marshal himself was not averse to collecting credit among his friends for this supposition. But even a casual analysis of the char-acters of those involved rules out this belief. It was with Darlan, not with Hitler, that the Marshal was forced to bargain.

The status eventually occupied by Darlan in the regime of the new chief of state was a further proof of this bargaining. Pierre Laval, under the Marshal, ranked as vice chief of state, but it was Darlan, who stood lower in the hierarchy, who was officially proclaimed heir to the Marshal. Why, if Laval were second in command, should a technical subordinate be chosen as official successor to the chief? The reason was that Darlan still had something to sell whereas Laval had nothing. Darlan was engaged in bartering away the fleet on an installment plan which left him free to withhold the prize at the last moment or to press for immediate settlement at the moment of his choosing. It is one of the minor ironies of the war that he lived neither to succeed to an old man lingering on borrowed time nor to realize his reward for trading the fleet to the more likely victors.

In order to preserve the fleet and the remaining colonies, at the moment for Vichy, in the long run as his principal stocks in trade, the Admiral was careful to place in all the key positions lieutenants of his own choosing and upon whose personal loyalty he could depend. An admiral of his making was in the colonial ministry, another in the government of Tunisia, another at Martinique and still another, later on, in Indo-China.*

For a time the administrative side of the Vichy government appeared to consist almost entirely of navy personnel. The army lost the day, as Otto Abetz had reminded General de la Laurencie, and the navy, secure in its position of courted

---

* Those interested in the trivia of history may reflect at some future date upon the ubiquity in this war of land-based seamen. Admirals and administrative navy officials have occupied a disproportionate place in the intrigues and strategies of the landsmen. Entirely apart from Darlan and his assemblage of naval politicians there have been Admirals Leahy and Standley, Horthy, Robert, to say nothing of the two former naval chiefs of their respective countries, Messrs. Churchill and Roosevelt.

favorite, was triumphant in its technical unconquerability. It was a fact, of course, that the fleet had faced none of the terrible ordeals which had routed the army. It had fought well where fighting had been indicated, but it simply had not been forced to engage any foe of comparable strength. Thus it remained one source of pride still open to the bewildered and unhappy French people.

And so, in harmony with the wishes of Hitler, Pétain with Darlan remained master of the fleet and of such of the colonies as had not decided to ally themselves with De Gaulle. Now three ambitions had to be reconciled, three strong wills brought into harmony. For Darlan the problem was simple. He wanted power upon the Marshal's death and he felt that day to be not too far distant. He therefore resolved to do nothing in the interim which might displease either the Marshal or the still more powerful Fuehrer.

Hitler's objectives varied. His first phase, which lasted from the June of France's collapse until November of the same year, was one of wishing to woo and reassure the British. Until October he remained convinced that a peace by negotiation could still be secured if only Churchill could be replaced by one or other of the appeasers. This was the period in which he felt that any increase in German sea power would frighten those Englishmen who might be persuaded that England could exist in a world of German ambition. Had he been successful here, the crushing of Russia could have proceeded according to schedule and the question of naval supremacy would have settled itself in due time. But, from November on, the Fuehrer recognized that the war would be long, that neither friendly approaches nor horrifying bombings were affecting the determination of Great Britain. Now he began to think that insistence upon a seizure of the fleet would be

wisest. There was still time, and little difficulty would have
been made by the Marshal, provided he could meanwhile
have squared matters with Darlan. But this time the objec-
tions came from the German Admiralty itself. It was impossible, felt these men, to count upon the rank and file of the
French sailors to man the ships under German direction—or
even under French direction if that seemed to them contrary
to the best interests of France.* But the provision of German
sailors to man these ships would have meant a tremendous
strain upon Germany's reserve of skilled seamen and would
have produced far more inconvenience than advantage. At
least fifty thousand sailors would have been needed to remove
the ships from their berths, plus six months of expensive
training, the necessary consumption of fuel oil which could
at that time ill be spared, of ammunition and possibly of lives.
This human and material force already was proving its maxi-
mum value in the opinion of Germany's naval strategists, in
the intensification of submarine warfare then under way.
Admiral Raeder preferred operating his six hundred submarines to placing the same number of men upon sixty
cruisers or destroyers not nearly so useful in the ultimate
prosecution of the war.

But Hitler's second inspiration was better than the first.
He enlisted the aid of Marshal Pétain in an excellently conceived blackmail scheme. Playing first one and then the other,
the objective being to obtain concessions not otherwise
granted to enemies open or tacit, the Marshal and the Fuehrer
saw how they might obtain first from England, then from
the United States, favors contingent upon the continued
immobility of the fleet. For two years this vague threat that

---

* Desertions from the *Richelieu* in New York early in 1943 prove the correctness of this estimate.

the weight of fleet and colonies might be thrown into the scales against the Allies was used to obtain a series of favors and concessions ordinarily inconceivable from belligerents at war with the conquerors of the favored nation.

Thus the Marshal permitted the systematic looting of France's farms and food supplies, in contemptuous excess of anything provided by the terms of the armistice. But he demanded, and with querulous insult where reluctance was manifested, that the Allies replace the foodstuffs from which their enemies had benefited. Insistently he required that France, which under his dominance treated the Allies in all respects as enemies with which it was engaged in undeclared war, receive the careful courtesy accorded a neutral nation. Belgium, Holland, Norway, Denmark, all were treated by Britain and the United States as involuntary appendages of the enemy. In this respect their position was identical with that of France. And yet France demanded and in large measure, thanks to the blackmail weapon so skillfully employed, received the food and supplies which were denied by right to other occupied countries and sent only to Sweden, Switzerland and Portugal, states of whose neutrality there could be no doubt.

It was to the interest of Hitler and the Marshal that he be permitted to create the fiction of an independent and free France functioning on Vichy's side of the demarcation line; a France perfectly free to get in or to stay out of war, to negotiate her own agreements and to conclude deals as she chose with Germany on the one side and with the Allies, individually and collectively, on the other.

The British, to whom the realities of war came earlier and more sternly, were disposed to treat this presumptuousness with the coolness it deserved. Understanding the strength

and disposition of the fleet and something of conditions in
the colonies, and being bound, moreover, to the Frenchmen
who in the darkest hour of the war had decided to sink or
swim with England, she had no inclination to continue a
meek acquiescence in the ignoring of her powerful blockade
which the Marshal continued to demand.

With the United States, matters were different. The nation
was not then at war and was insulated both by geography
and viewpoint from the currents threatening to engulf
Europe. Furthermore the strong sentimental attachment
uniting the two countries, dating back to the very infancy
of the American republic, made genuinely painful to most
people the possibility of an open breach. This attachment was
aided in confusing the issues for the American people by the
temperament and associations of many powerful American
connections with France. It is difficult for honest and sympathetic people to believe that sentiments which are in essence
traitorous would originate with charming and intelligent men.
Old soldiers and sailors, enthusiastic young diplomats, saw
the old Marshal through a pleasing mist of legend and sentiment. Since even few Frenchmen knew the reality of his
close and secretive nature, it was not readily discernible to
foreigners and most of them proved as easily influenced by
legend as the pathetic Frenchmen who had been betrayed
by it.

A combination of forces prevailed upon the United States
to see Vichy and its ruler with a far more lenient and trust-
ing eye than those closer to the uglier reality were disposed to
afford. Wishing to believe that at last France, the true France,
would return through the Marshal as a penitent to those who
loved her, it was easy for these influences to feel that kind-
ness, the provision of a shipload of grain here, or of oil there,

would be far more effective than gruff refusal and that, further-more, the old Marshal who was resisting by heaven knew what braveries the Nazi pressure to obtain French ships, the important strategic bases of the Western Hemisphere, the territories and resources of the colonial empire, would be strengthened in his resolve by these tangible evidences of friendly good will from across the ocean. In thus implying that the Marshal's noble behavior might be influenced by material considerations these reasoners were not, of course, precisely flattering the moral judgment of the old man. But nations, like men who decide upon a course of action, some-times are curiously obstinate in justifying themselves with a variety of reasons, some of them inevitably contradictory.

And so the Marshal, backed by American policy against British judgment, was able to obtain almost all that his heart desired. He was treated as the head of a state, as a friend and equal of the United States. He was permitted to import, with a freedom forced upon the reluctant British, a variety of raw materials and foodstuffs of which his ally and master Hitler was able to skim off a rich eighty per cent to rebuild his depleted imports. The real French people, for whose sake the United States was willing to weaken the British blockade, actually were just as impoverished as though the blockade were applied with full severity. But with a curious blindness the United States, which for years had had the best oppor-tunity of all to learn the terrible object lessons of appeasement, continued to behave as though its food and oil really did benefit the poor French peasant, the struggling industrialist, instead of the man now engaged in crushing the heart and soul out of France.

There is available on this point the testimony of a qualified American observer, the Rev. Howard L. Brooks, a Unitarian minister who has embodied in his book, *Prisoners of Hope*, his experiences of more than a year spent in striving to ameliorate the plight of the children of France. Mr. Brooks thus describes his experience in buying bread made from flour sent into France through the American Red Cross:

This white bread was distributed on Sunday, May 25, and on the two following Sundays, by fifteen thousand bakeries in unoccupied France. I had heard that the Red Cross officials had worked out a detailed plan. The French people were to be informed that this bread was a gift from the American people. It was to be a real gift; that is, it would be given free and no bread cards would be surrendered for it. In other words, it was to be an addition to the legal ration. That, at least, was the program worked out between the representatives of the American Red Cross and officials of the Vichy government.

The negotiations were extraordinarily involved. There is no doubt that Vichy was striving to weaken the propagandistic effect such an action would undoubtedly have. But I did not know how successful the Vichy people had been until I got my loaf of bread.

At the markets and in the bakeries where the bread was being distributed, you saw large posters reading: "Free gift from the American people to the French people." And it was not without some pride that I entered the bakery in the Rue Dugommier and asked for my loaf. I didn't have to tell the salesgirl that I was American. She recognized my accent. She looked at me sullenly. Then she said: "Your bread card, Monsieur?"

Wondering, I gave it to her. "But I thought . . ."

She tore off the coupons. "We all thought," she told me. Then she handed me the loaf. "Here, take your bread card. I hope you realize what your countrymen have done to us."

I wanted to say something but was too astonished to be able to speak.

"We all know you Americans have a lot of money and are so very generous with it," the girl said and stared into my eyes. "But we didn't know you could be quite so cruel. Was it really necessary to make poor people give up their bread cards? After all, I suppose it is good propaganda. But there's no doubt that the Nazis will benefit by it. They'll get the equivalent of the flour the Americans have sent."

Then I began to understand.

In spite of the careful arrangements that the agents of the American Red Cross had made, the Vichy crew had succeeded in double-crossing them. Vichy, at first, had allowed the hungry people of France to hope. They said that the bread would be given out free. Then, at the last minute, the government decided that though the bread would be distributed free, bread cards would have to be given up for it. Therefore the actual result of all the complicated negotiations was that no Frenchman got an ounce of bread more than he would have got anyway.

Vichy explained to the Red Cross that at the moment there was not as much bread in France as there were bread cards. They protested that everyone would get his proper ration only if the American bread were included in the rations. Naturally there is no proof available that this was a lie. But even if there were not enough bread, it still might have been better if we had not sent any to

be given away without cards. Then the people would have
seen who was taking away their bread. Then the people
would have been able to see that Vichy was sending
so much flour to Germany that not even enough for
their miserable rations was left. But this is just what
Vichy wanted to avoid, and succeeded. As it was, the
distribution of bread turned out to be propaganda for
Vichy.

The American officials could do nothing. No one
could do anything. And a great many Frenchmen were
very bitter about it. Most people realized that America
did not intend the Nazis to get more flour, but that was
the actual result.

The United States continued also to treat with a curious
and disheartening deference such petty colonial sub-dictators
as Admiral Robert in Martinique, Admiral Decoux in Indo-
China, Admiral Godefroy in Alexandria, while refusing to
risk incurring the annoyance of the exacting vanquished by
showing aid or even courtesy to the forces of Frenchmen who
had continued the fight. Even when they used the bases made
available by De Gaullist occupation of possessions in Oceania,
the Indian Ocean and the Gulf of New Guinea, members of
the United States services behaved as though forced by a
national policy of appeasement to do so, with an almost
apologetic furtiveness containing little gratitude or comrade-
liness but only an implied regret that these bounties were not
being made available by the other side.

This policy was given a seeming justification at the time of
the November invasion when Admiral Darlan, who suddenly
saw a better chance of success with the growing strength of
the Allies than he did as the imprisoned successor of an old

man who seemed bent on living forever, suddenly agreed to join forces with the American invaders of North Africa. Its apologists seemed bent upon turning the great opportunist into the very model of a patriot and upon speaking as though every end and aim of American policy had been to bring about this eventuality. The case is a difficult one to make, and it is not helped by the fact that in thus praising the Admiral and his corps of hand-picked seekers after the main chance, the United States succeeded for a time in dividing Frenchmen fighting for liberation into two seemingly irreconcilable camps.

But up until this seventh of November, Hitler and Pétain had good reason to be proud of the success of their plan. The blackmail was paying double dividends, with Pétain receiving all of the personal honors and prestige for which his soul had long thirsted, and Hitler, the realist, receiving the information relayed from a dozen important Vichyite listening posts in the New World, was able also to send, via the messengers so thoughtfully provided by the New World at the listening post of Vichy, just those messages he deemed most useful to his continued success, and was in addition the pleased and voracious recipient of valuable supplies for the use of his war machine.

Consider this list of goods sent from southeastern France alone into Germany for the one month of June 1942. It is extracted from a confidential list sent to agents of the French National Railway Corporations:

Oats, straw and hay	25,000	tons
Vegetables, fruit	24,000	"
Wine	60,000	"
Frames for cars and tractors	25,000	"
Steel, cast iron, iron bars	13,300	"

Copper, brass, tin	10,600	tons
Pyrites	11,000	"
Beams	10,000	"
Chestnut and oak logs	53,000	"
Wheat	55,000	"
Hides, leather, shoes	2,300	"
Nitrogen	34,500	"

In another single shipment which the British had tried unavailingly to halt were seven million pounds of rubber. American insistence finally sent this upon its way to Marseille where the customary substantial proportion found its way to German trucks and tanks.

But, with the landing in North Africa, Hitler's interest in the comparatively minor pickings of blackmail waned abruptly. Now his own Mediterranean supply lines were in actual danger and a direct threat was in the making against the armies of General Rommel. To enable this force to fight as long a delaying battle as possible, it was necessary that Hitler should end the farce of occupied and unoccupied France with the Marshal's make-believe rulership and that he should finally obtain full and unrestricted use of the idle French ships.

And so, at last, Hitler brushed aside what remained of the fiction of the armistice and marched in upon the puppet principality of Vichy. All deference forgotten, the Marshal found himself treated at last as one with the other quislings who had aided Hitler's rise. For the first time he acknowledged a reason for anger with Hitler.

France's martyrdom of two years had failed to arouse him. The execution of hostages, the steady robbery of peasant and manufacturer alike, the forced drain of workers, the hope long deferred of prisoner releases, the suppression of civil liberties and the endless, alien presence of the spying conqueror—all of these sorrows and indignities could be lumped together under the general heading of expiation for the sins of the Republic. But the careless brushing aside of his authority, the open contempt for the state of which for so brief a time he had been master—these were intolerable for the old man.

There was, for a moment, a shadow of resistance. He might, like Darlan, have proclaimed a holy war. He might even have retrieved some remnants of that soldier's honor of which he once had been so proud. But a conversation with that shrewd and practical peasant, Pierre Laval, changed his mind, showed the pitfalls of this sudden impulse to appeal at last to the people for resistance. Apart from the tragedy of armed repulse for this suicidal move, urged Laval, there would be the disgrace, the triumph for critics and renegade Frenchmen, of a public confession by its instigator and chief signatory, that the armistice had been a mistake and a trap for the misled people of France. It would mean the end, in sorry confusion, of all the dreams of the patriarchal state, the garden spot of the New Order. And it would mean the end of the Marshal as father confessor and benevolent despot over the millions of his penitent and toiling countrymen.

Like the gambler seeking to recoup part of his loss, the Marshal already had staked more and still more of France's substance upon the eventual triumph of Hitler. And now, after a brief flare of anger and dismay, he was ready to stake a little more, to continue in the fiction that all was well rather than to admit his errors and to confess to the world that he had led his people into an unending slavery.

As a sop to the wounded pride of this ancient, Hitler promised that the seizure of unoccupied France and the suppression of the Marshal's authority by Marshal Gerd von

Runstedt should be atoned for by a pledge to respect the neutrality of a small zone around Toulon, the naval base sheltering what now remained of the once proud French fleet. Absurd as this small concession was, it was respected for only a few days. Its purpose was merely to disarm the suspicions of the fleet until Hitler himself was ready for its surprise seizure. He wished first to establish a chain of military airports all around the fortified roadways of Toulon. He wanted to recall the submarines now prowling the Atlantic so that they could provide an armed wall across the port channel and thus prevent any mass flight of the vessels, disarmed, run down and inadequately equipped, but still representing, with their crews, a formidable aggregation of naval might.

There was time to save this fleet. But its heads waited stupidly for orders from Vichy which never came; as though from Vichy they expected at last a bold initiative which would put honor and the national interest first! So they waited, preparing neither for escape nor for combat. And, when it spoke from Algiers, even the voice of Darlan, the respected and beloved admiral to whom most of the commanders owed personally their present positions, was incompetent to move them. Once again the seven stars of a marshal had proved superior in the minds of the tradition-bound professionals of the navy to the mere five stars of an admiral of the fleet. And simple sailors, asking with increasing tension for permission to get under way, met only the reply, day after day: "We are waiting for orders from above."

The orders never came. And it was the initiative of subalterns and petty officers alone which made possible the last tragic resort of suicide for the brave ships of the home base. Pro-Vichyites at the base had prepared well for a possible attempt at flight by their underlings. All crew members capable of maneuvering the vessels had been sent on shore to defend the fortifications of the city, thus unmanning the ships. But, immediately the Germans stormed the city, the sailors who had been sent to the fortresses were ordered back on board by their officers. Thus the fight was abandoned at the gates of the city, but the sailors rushing back on board were left without the ghost of a chance to get their ships under steam in time for an effective escape, since the Germans actually were treading on their heels the whole way back.

If the admirals had not wanted to fight there was no need of their taking crews from the men-of-war, cruisers and fortresses for defense of the fortifications. The practical effect of their action was to make it impossible for the crews, whose loyalty to France rather than to Vichy was the weak link in the plotters' chain, either to fight for the preservation of their ships or to escape with them to sea. But the plot had been foreseen by a few resourceful subordinates and for days they had prepared in secret, as a desperate last measure, for the scuttling of the ships.

The brave sailors with the little red pompons were ready for any deed which would have preserved their ships for action against the real enemy. They were ready to fight, to run the gauntlet out to sea, to die readily for a chance to rejoin the allies of France. But this tame submission that they now realized was contemplated by their commanders was intolerable. They determined that their ships should never fall into German hands.

When with a common accord they embarked upon their tragic task, time had to be found in which the waiting German soldiers would be distracted and delayed. It takes time, and huge quantities of water, to kill a ship. And this time was purchased in blood and suffering by the heroic civilian workmen of the arsenal of Toulon. Weapons from secret caches, cobblestones torn from the street, trucks capsized to form makeshift barricades, all were used against the surprised German soldiers, whose orders were to be on the lookout for disorder from the ships but who had received no warning of an uprising on the land. They had expected no more than a token resistance from a few disorderly sailors on the ships, since the fleet already had been promised by Vichy's admirals. Startled and angered, they were forced to battle for several hours against the workers. And during the relentless massacre which followed, the thunder of successive explosions in the harbor told of the disappearance, one after the other, of the proud vessels of France's navy.

Many Frenchmen were killed in this effort, and survivors of the riot were captured by thousands, to disappear later into the bloody mystery of the German torture camps. But the name of France won back part of its lost luster from the deeds of these men and of the nameless sailors who took part in this gallant and despairing gesture.

By thus choosing death by drowning, the fleet escaped the fate of having to prolong still further France's long enslavement. But it escaped also the opposite alternative. Had the officers obeyed Admiral Darlan the ships could have escaped to Bizerte before the Germans were prepared to halt them, and there have become a part in the great Allied effort which won back North Africa. The mystery here is the behavior of Admiral de Laborde, who might have chosen to obey Darlan, actually his superior although possessing only the same five stars. By disregarding the orders from Algiers he may merely have been demonstrating his respect for an authority superior to that of the Admiral. Or he may possibly have felt that, with Darlan now on the side of the

Fuehrer's enemy, his own chances of succession to the promises made to the former were considerably brighter. He may
have felt that there was plenty of reason left still for an
ambitious man to gamble upon the rewards that Hitler might
bestow. Or he might, animated by the fatalism of officers
who can imagine no alternative to the respect for rank imbued
within the traditional service careerist of both army and navy,
have felt that while Pétain still outranked Darlan, he, the
subordinate of both of them, had no right to ignore the elder
in favor of the younger.

With the fleet gone, the African squadrons partly destroyed, the surviving ships racing to join with the rest of
the colonies in the growing might of the United Nations,
Pétain the would-be dictator, the almost successful black-
mailer, found himself disarmed. Under the growing pressures
of war, the partnership with Hitler, once promising such
glory, was rapidly crumbling. The old man who had sacrificed
all for power now found that power waning like a candle in
the sun.

CHAPTER 10

THE INDICTMENT

FROM THE HEIGHTS of Verdun to the depths of Vichy, the road taken by Marshal Pétain was steep and well marked. Its beginnings were to be found back in the far-off days of L'Ecole Supérieure de Guerre, in the famous feud of machine gun versus bayonet.

The road took a sharp downward turn when, the elderly colonel-instructor having metamorphosed into the comparatively young general, the desperate struggle of Verdun had begun to merit its awful fame as one of history's bloodiest battles. This terrible test of the defensive was not ended until, Pétain still refusing to counterattack the besieging army, General Nivelle superseded him and brought the long agony to an end. This was an indignity that cut deep into the proud and obstinate soul, and the hurt was made worse when this interloper became generalissimo and Pétain was passed over. The bloody failure of Nivelle should have assuaged the slight in some measure, since it became necessary for the War Ministry to retreat with some embarrassment and to offer supreme command to the man they had first passed over.

But Pétain was not an officer to be forgiving toward second choosers and he merely swallowed resentment without digesting it. However, for one and a half years he was master of the French Army and was able to experiment endlessly with defensive tactics. And then, through the interference of the British, he was again deprived of a supreme honor. His subordinate and erstwhile superior, General Foch, became interallied commander-in-chief and, through a series of dogged attacks, succeeded in ending the war victoriously.

It was during this war that Pétain first became the fanatical apologist of defensive tactics and thus conclusively proved his own limitations as an expert in the science of war. For wars are not won wholly defensively or wholly offensively. The brilliant general is the one who knows when and in what proportion to mix these mutually indispensable strategies and who has never let himself be seduced into favoring one at the expense of the other. Consistently Marshal Pétain has refused to admit that war, just as any other science, must keep pace with the march of time and invention. From an evolutionary process he wished to crystallize a permanently hardened method of war, oblivious to change except in minor details and fought perpetually upon a field where the enemy invariably attacks with terrific losses while the defender wins by firing from his hole.

This obsession, plus the unforgiving conviction that he had been slighted and passed over for lesser men, helped carry the Marshal almost insensibly over many a mile of his downhill road. At first without conscious planning, but with the background realization of the likelihood of war which is part of the equipment of every military professional, the Marshal felt that the next struggle might see France fighting a war wholly according to his theories, and fighting it successfully. For a decade following the end of the last war, the French Army in equipment and training was the finest on the

Continent. The Germans, on the other hand, had no army left to speak of and were not being encouraged to work for one. But the Marshal was not above a small hope that this condition would not always obtain, that sooner or later Germany's armies would reorganize and expand and that Germany's suicidal ambition would send her once again over the French frontiers, there to be annihilated by the perfect organization of French defense.

Given this frame of mind, the slow disintegration of the French Army was not so difficult to understand. So long as there was no potential foe for the French to fight, continued high expenditures for the maintenance of a large army in perfect fighting trim began to seem unwarranted and certainly were not politically popular. And so the Marshal permitted French superiority to melt by almost imperceptible degrees, while not considering it particularly worth while to rebuke the stealthy moves by which Germany moved once again in the direction of rearmament. The gap was still wide, and only by permitting the Germans to build enough of an army to push into the French trap could this still visionary defensive experiment someday become an actual and resounding success.

Thus the military pre-eminence bequeathed by Foch quietly rusted or rotted away while Germany—unhampered by outworn tradition or a false sense of safe superiority—patiently began to create its own offensive machine from the ground up. Indeed, Pétain actually encouraged this creation, since he condoned successive violations of disarmament clauses in the Versailles Treaty and, later, when Hitler's shrewd plans were beginning to materialize, wholeheartedly supported Flandin in his tolerance of the Rhineland reoccupation. Still later he upheld Daladier and Air General Vuillemin,* the appeasers of Munich, in the face of an earnest recommendation by General Gamelin, his own creature, for an immediate preventive war.

So that, if France slipped low while Germany became powerful, a large share of the blame must go to the stupid egotism of a man who did not mind seeing his country attacked by an army as strong as or stronger than her own, so long as that attack brought an opportunity for vindication of his pet theories. Even had he been right and France emerged victorious, his responsibility would have been grievous. But disaster more terrible than any previous event in his country's long history has resulted from his obstinacy, his blindness, and his determination to see in the hereditary enemies of his country merely the useful adjuncts of his own climb to power.

As responsible head of the French Army until 1934, as Minister of War in 1934, as authoritative adviser to the leading statesmen, as guide and protector of his two successors in office, General Maurin and Colonel Fabry, and of his own pupil Daladier, the ill-fated Bull of Vaucluse, what one man in the past quarter century of French history can claim a greater share of responsibility for the sorry plight of the nation's armies, for the fact that a great and powerful enemy prepared itself down to the last detail for conquest and the annihilation of France, without one word of protest or warning being uttered to stay its course or to warn the people of what might lie ahead?

Furthermore the Marshal detested the Third Republic and all of the constant, vociferous and self-seeking turmoil

---

* In 1943 General Vuillemin, who since 1940 had remained idle in Africa, volunteered to serve under de Gaulle in whatever capacity he might be needed. He cheerfully agreed to serve in the only post available, and became a lieutenant-colonel with the forces of General Le Clerc.

of political rivalry. He found it fatally easy to persuade himself, and to listen to the persuasions of others, that all of the ills of France were traceable to the Republic. From that it was merely a step to the belief that whoever worked to overthrow the Republic would be performing a patriotic service for France. And, like a too enthusiastic medical experimenter, he was not wholly averse to killing the patient in his determination to be rid of the disease. Here again the plight of France's armies did not seem to him necessarily an evil thing. Military reverses, the incapacity of armies either to stem civilian disorder or to repel invasion from without, notoriously are the aids of revolution at home. And with revolts, he had the assurance of the friends who hated the Republic as sincerely as he did, would come their chance to be rid once and for all of parliamentary government and to establish the Marshal as head of France's first experiment with modern authoritarianism. Since this aim would have also the powerful backing of the men who were building the armies which alone were likely to attack France, here was additional reason for turning a blind eye to the terrifying thoroughness of their preparations and for hoping, without thinking of the implications of that hope, that when the great armies did at last swing into motion their power would be behind the ambitions of the Marshal and not against him.

The downhill passage during these past ten years or so has been swift and uninterrupted. In these years the personal considerations which might seem understandable in younger, less successful men, took precedence over all matters of a higher duty, and over the customary serenities of great age. It was as though the Marshal, conscious of the swift passing of his borrowed years, was obsessed with the need for realizing before the end something of the satisfactions of unlimited power. In this he was not cynical as a franker man might have been. His words and his actions in this period are clothed in righteousness, in the sincerity of self-persuasion. But, as many another ambitious meddler with destiny has discovered, events are not so easily controlled as thoughts are. The will to defeat an attacking army from fortresses of steel and concrete passed by almost unrecognizable degrees into the will to tolerate a small defeat for the good of the soul of France. But defeat by the armies he had permitted the Germans to amass could never be small; neither could the ambitions nourished by the German masters be satisfied with a small defeat. The little lesson turned into great rout, the rout into collapse, the collapse into catastrophe final and irretrievable. Far worse than the Marshal's muddled dream was the deadly reality for which he was now responsible.

Marshal Pétain had been dispatched in the service of his country to win the new government of Spain into a friendly relationship with France. But instead of fulfilling this mission, difficult enough in view of the outspoken sympathies of the French people with Franco's opponents in the civil war, the Marshal used his old friendship and present prestige with the Caudillo to reach upon his own account a harmonious understanding with the master totalitarian of them all, Adolf Hitler. The Marshal willingly exposed the weaknesses of his own nation and people to the merciless gaze of these potential enemies in order that he personally might be assured of their help and backing when the time came to foment disorders within France. Thus he personally established sympathetic understanding with Hitler for the eventual harming of France, and Hitler himself made known by the same intermediary his own satisfaction at the plans of France's best-known hero. The monster of Vichy was conceived at Burgos and Franco was the procurer who brought its parents together.

The unanimity with which it was recognized at Bordeaux that the Marshal was the one man who might obtain from Hitler concessions favorable to France was another indictment of the old man's conduct of recent years. It is not often that the best approach to a conqueror is through the military chieftain and political head of the defeated nation. Recognition of his suitability for this mission was proof enough that the close relationship between the two had not worked for France's interest, and how little it has continued to do so France's plight today will eloquently attest.

The manner in which the Marshal used his newly acquired powers was evidence enough of the premeditated nature of his agreements with Hitler. He dismissed the Parliament. He gave the country no opportunity to discuss or even to know the real terms of the armistice. He alone concluded the bargain which sold France into slavery and his alone must be the responsibility for the terrible toll that his willing compliance has exacted. He need not be judged too harshly for asking an armistice. France's plight at this time was such that it could not matter much whether she asked for a respite, à la Pétain, or capitulated in the field, à la Leopold III. And it was impossible for the average Frenchman, be he civilian or soldier, to believe passionately in the strength of British resistance or to foresee the day when the Soviet state would reverse its stand and engage the Hitlerian might with a juggernaut of its own. But Leopold, who also was overwhelmed, was no friend to the conqueror. Although lavish promises were made to induce him to represent Nazi domination within his conquered country, he steadfastly refused, proudly remaining prisoner in a country of prisoners. He was forced to take Belgium from the war, but the honor of his country remained intact. Whereas the Marshal not only negotiated with the conquerors, he fraternized with them. Everything, including the good name and the very life of France, went to purchase him the honors of a puppet dictator in an enslaved nation.

On June 19, 1940, the Marshal assembled the members of his personal following (Darlan had joined it only on the evening of the previous day) and communicated to them the news of the negotiations proceeding tortuously via Burgos and Madrid. Hitler had refused to make known all of the armistice conditions, but he did divulge one. And obviously, this one, to the Marshal, outweighed all of the unknown and unguessable exactions ahead. The point the Fuehrer was willing to concede was this: provided the two groups could reach an agreement upon which fighting could cease, he would not insist upon occupying the whole of France. There would be a partitioning line around an unoccupied region, the general boundaries of which already seemed fairly well known to the Marshal. And within the line a French government could function, limitedly, perhaps, and subject to spying control, but nevertheless a government with which Pétain and his friends could play their long-awaited game of dictatorship.

The Reichschancellor knew his men. For the sake of this illusion of sovereignty, Pétain for power and the others for profit could be made to swallow almost any indignity for the nation as a whole.

Again the comparison with Leopold must be made. The latter signed no agreement, willingly forfeited his crown and his power rather than seem to his people a willing collaborator. When a new Nazi order against Belgians must be promulgated, he issues it under orders, not as a free agent. But in

France, all of the Fuehrer's wishes were willingly disseminated in the name of the Marshal. All of the robbery, the shootings, the seizure of hostages was done in the name of Marshal Pétain, although the deeds were those designated by Hitler. Thus the pitiful blackmail was perpetrated upon the French, who obeyed many an unpalatable injunction because of their pity for an old man whom the enemy might punish. And the Marshal's steady stream of propaganda—for he was an apt pupil of Dr. Goebbels—kept them thus deceived, sorrowing for him, unaware that this very docility of theirs had been sold to the enemy as part of the price for the Marshal's ability to issue decrees.

Why did the Marshal accede so readily, and lend his name to many an order which he knew full well must anger his people and contribute in time to a breakdown of his influence over them? Largely because he could not feel himself as fortunate as King Leopold who was able to resign his throne secure in the knowledge that no interloper was likely to seize it from him. But the Marshal, himself a usurper, must be constantly on guard lest one of his watchful subordinates excel him in amenability and thus win away the power for which he sacrificed so much. Constantly he had to take care that none should outbid him in traitorous courtesies; that Hitler should not feel that another might handle the French people with greater skill than he. Hitler proved an insatiable master.

But how did the proud Pétain, who found obedience to a Clemenceau, a Joffre, a Foch, so intolerable, so readily obey a Hitler, who certainly has no more claim upon obedience from a soldier than they? In the first place Hitler had no associations with the hated trappings of the Republic, and indeed had proved himself the master of the parliamentarians of his own country, having set a good example in this respect for the Marshal to follow. Since he possessed so many of the attributes of mind the Marshal admires, it was natural that the old soldier should mentally invest the Fuehrer with an extra star for his sleeve, thus making him in effect a sort of marshal of Europe and therefore entitled by military etiquette to command a lesser marshal of France and his seven stars. But in addition to these rather hazy self-justifications, there was also the influential fact that Hitler did not scruple to use many indirect weapons to force obedience from his underlings, whereas the Frenchmen with whom the Marshal had dealt during the rest of his long life had for the most part been restrained by a natural courtesy or by the respect soldiers accord to one another from blunt pressures of the type which seemed so natural to the conquerors.

But, while the Marshal for one reason or another seemed reasonably subject to Nazi control, he in turn extended the severest control and exacted the sharpest obedience from all the millions of Frenchmen whom he regarded as his subordinates. And in many cases the demands of Hitler accorded perfectly with his own wishes. In the matter of the Riom trials for instance, nothing could have suited the old man better than to have the personal stage-managing of this business of apportioning blame for the war and the defeat. Hitler saw the propaganda value of persuading Frenchmen to believe that responsibility for their present plight rested wholly upon the shoulders of other Frenchmen. Marshal Pétain saw the aid to his personal prestige bound to accrue if he could prove that the agents and creatures of popular government had brought about these defeats and disasters in spite of his own wisdom and warning. For Hitler the foregone result of the trials could be a prelude to new and still harsher exactions. For Pétain the result would vindicate his demand that France

and a part of their love even of France itself. Following the
Stavisky scandal, Chautemps convinced many people that if
popular government were to be merely a matter of exchange
between his corrupt followers and the equally venal friends of
Albert Sarraut, then it would be just as well if popular government were superseded by some stronger force.

Chautemps was one of the most accomplished opportunists
in the great era of opportunism. Having shaken the nation's
faith in the Radicals to its foundations, he nevertheless was
skillful enough to return as premier during the era of the
Popular Front and to cultivate during these days the men who
were grooming the Marshal for his role. Chautemps, having
dealt so grave a blow, could foresee the probable end of parliamentary government and so was ready and assiduous in his
attentions to the most likely future rulers of France. When
Blum overlooked the Cagoulard plot in which Pétain was so
gravely implicated, he did it because his kindly heart was
persuaded that the Marshal was merely the tool of cleverer
men and had no real vice of unpatriotism. But Chautemps,
who was premier at the time, had shrewder reasons for for-
bearance and was able later to turn them to better advantage
than could the generous honesty of Léon Blum.

And in Bordeaux, and Vichy in 1940, Chautemps appeared
to claim his reward, while those who had worked with him
and under him in the earlier years received theirs in a prison
cell. But Blum may well be right. It is entirely conceivable
that, between the souls of the men silenced and chained by
Vichy and that of their companion who so prudently secured
his own freedom and comfort in the United States, the advantage is with the prisoners.

But there were others besides Chautemps whose absence
from the dock at Riom was remarkable and revelatory. The

same Flandin and Laval who ranged themselves self-righteously upon the side of the accusers could have been asked some pointed questions had they too been subjected to the inquisitorial ordeal imposed upon their fellows.

There is a curious chain of coincidence following from the association of these two with Pétain in the Doumergue Cabinet of 1934. Every move of Hitler's since that date appears to have been timed to take strategic advantage of the position in France of one or other of these two accomplices. It was Flandin who soothed and controlled French reaction to the news of Hitler's beginning air force, nucleus of the later mighty Luftwaffe. It was Flandin again who minimized the implications of the Saar plebiscite and the barrage of German propaganda which preceded it. It was Laval who controlled France when Mussolini attacked Ethiopia and sponsored the accompanying anti-British propaganda aimed at weakening England's empire, thus undermining Franco-British relations without bringing any major improvement in Italo-French understanding. It was Flandin who furnished Germany with a pretext, which most of her appeasers accepted as valid, for re-establishing compulsory military service, by doubling the duration of France's conscription term just one day before the German announcement. And it was Flandin who, upon Hitler's first open act of provocation, the march on the Rhineland, silenced the dismay of the French people and let the time for action slip irretrievably by.

When the elections of 1936 rendered both of these assiduous collaborationists temporarily powerless, Hitler looked elsewhere for the same brand of co-operation. He found it, probably upon recommendation, with Georges Bonnet. Bonnet was powerless as an influence upon the French people, but his usefulness was in reporting to Hitler upon the prob-

obvious to the world and his own countrymen almost since his first emergence upon the political stage. If anything, he is the more honorable of the two, since the Marshal's betrayals have been wrapped in a mantle of self-righteousness, have scarcely been acknowledged even to himself as the falsities they are but always presented as the holy admonitions of a man consciously better than his neighbors and determined to recall them to the knowledge of their sins.

Laval has never troubled to hide his motives. Even before the first World War he was recognized as a potential menace to the national security. His name could be found upon the infamous "Register B" wherein every line contained the name of a man who would be placed under arrest on the day of mobilization. He saved himself in this instance by forsaking his accomplices and thus becoming a double betrayer. He emerged from the war a rich man, as cured of the socialism which had first elected him as the Socialists were of him. And since those days he had never concealed his preoccupation with German and Italian interests, nor his somewhat incoherent plans for a Latin-nation coalition which would oppose Soviet materialism and the supposedly allied forces of democratic government with a clerico-fascist dictatorship upon the pattern which General Franco was hopefully and bloodily struggling to inaugurate. His close associates in many plots for their mutual enrichment were the amnestied traitors Caillaux and Malvy. Each of his cabinets brought new advantages to the enemies of France, new losses to his country's chances of future peace and victory, and new millions to the bank deposits of Pierre Laval. The French people as a whole had come to detest him; he had no political future and he knew that any further chance for power and continued enrichment depended entirely upon a German or Italian victory and the extent of his own usefulness to the conquerors.

Knowing all of this (and he knew it well), why did the Marshal make this frank opportunist, this prostitute politician, his friend, guide and political adviser, and later, when he rose precariously to power, alternately his scapegoat and his messenger?

The answer of the pro-Pétainists usually is to the effect that the Germans imposed Laval upon the Marshal, who nevertheless had bravely summoned courage to dismiss the odious little man in spite of the weight of German disapproval.

This contention also fails under the weight of dispassionate evidence. The Marshal has never once indicated that he disapproves of the policies, personal or political, of Pierre Laval. In most transactions they have acted together and with the implicit approval of one for the other. The Marshal's angry dismissal came, not as a consequence of some more than ordinarily base surrender of French sovereignty on the part of his vice chief but because the ambitious impatience of Laval became suddenly too apparent, too much of a threat to the continued rule of the ancient tyrant. Laval and his henchman, Marcel Déat, simply showed too plainly that they considered the Marshal's great age and his imperious demands for the deference ordinarily associated with royalty in the days when monarchs carried the power of life and death, to be both tiresome and unnecessary. They misjudged the power of his obstinacy, which had grown prodigiously by what it fed upon, and had taken the occasional appearance of senility for its actuality. The old man's formidable rage was instantly aroused. He determined to teach a lesson to any other possible aspirants to his throne and also to reinstate himself with the occupiers of France as the real fountainhead of decision and authority in case there were any lingering doubts in that quarter.

Prompt and effective the act may have been, and it gave the lie to many of the charitable rumors of senility and the innocent docility of an ancient dupe. But there was in it no vestige of patriotism nor of a belated care for France's pride. The issue was solely one of the wounded pride of the Marshal himself and it was resolved under German pressure and when the discarded adviser had wisely shown himself sufficiently impressed and abashed. Memoranda of the unfortunate General de la Laurencie, from which other quotations have been made, leave no doubt of this. The General recounts in some detail the sudden rift among the three men, and the part he and the German occupying authorities played in restoring peace once more among the jealous accomplices.

Déat has been arrested [said General de la Laurencie] for acts which were connected with domestic politics, most particularly his abusive newspaper campaigns like that of *L'Oeuvre* against the generals and personalities who enjoyed the confidence of the Marshal.

In any event I can affirm that any possible ministerial reshuffling will bring absolutely no change in the matter of the Montoire policy [collaboration] which still is unanimously that of the Minister [Laval] and other members of the government.

Laval has incurred disgrace at the hands of the chief of state, not because he announced himself in favor of collaboration, but because *his influence on domestic issues was becoming dangerous for the stability of the regime and was compromising the plan of national re-*

recovery undertaken by the Marshal. [Author's italics.]

The policy of collaboration, if we wish it to work in the interest of France as well as that of Germany, must be clean-cut, loyal and openly worked out, free from the sordid intrigues which delight those agents whose hearts are rotten, whose hands are soiled. . . .

A counselor of the German Embassy, Achenbach, commented: "France must choose between two policies, the one symbolized by De Gaulle—completely solidarity with England—or that of Montoire, collaboration with Germany, in which Laval is our best safeguard.

"The best for each of us would be that Laval be reintegrated in the Marshal's government and that he remain there until the peace treaty."

Abetz then added, with cynical cruelty:

"Kill him later, with a bullet in his belly. We will not care then."

. . . Laval's great mistake was that he did not know how, or he did not wish, to group back of the Marshal the partisans of the policy of collaboration.

This certainly is clear enough. It comes, moreover, from one of the Marshal's most devout admirers, a man whose single-minded interest at this time was to glorify the Marshal and his efforts at "recovery," and to advance his interests. It is interesting to note how strong a part German approval of Laval played in the eventual decision of the Marshal to restore his erstwhile friend. He might have resigned himself, rather than accept so distasteful a pressure. He might have demanded a more public confession of wrongdoing and penitence from the erring Laval. But he chose both to hang on and to be placated by the inexorable, steely pressure from

Paris. He took back his oily subordinate with a sigh, but he took him back.

Thus the rivalry was settled, by orders. And once the respective strength of each was understood by the other, the air remained clearer, the policy of collaboration proceeded more smoothly. It is significant that in the worst phases of the quarrel the Marshal never thought of taking against Pierre Laval the ferocious measures he had instituted against more patriotically disobedient Frenchmen. Laval was not denationalized, his fortune confiscated, as was the case with Giraud, Darlan and De Lattre de Tassigny. Even less was he condemned to death and to perpetual exile as were General de Gaulle and those who chose to stand with him.

But apologists of the Marshal are likely to continue their defense by instancing the supposed gains of collaboration, believing that by a patient bargaining in behalf of France treatment more favorable than that meted out to other conquered lands has been obtained. No belief could be more erroneous. By the spring of 1943 the number of Frenchmen shot as hostages by the Germans already exceeded twenty-five thousand. But the Belgians, unprotected by any such collaboration and probably equally outspoken in their distaste for the conqueror, have lost only around six hundred hostages. Even considering the considerable difference in population (and Belgium has only one fifth of the population of France), there still have been ten times as many French hostage-martyrs as Belgians. Where is the protection afforded by Vichy?

But with the growing strength of the United Nations, the Pétainists acquired new worries. The Marshal's only justification, and his one hope of continued immunity, lay in the continuance of the legend of German invincibility. For the practical followers of collaboration to its logical end, Hitler's continued and unchallenged success was a sine qua non. England, however, sturdily refused to die for the sake of the New Order, and the terrible, massed strength of Russia began to bleed white the once unconquerable German Army. The possibility of a future wherein Great Britain and Russia would re-establish democratic civilization in Europe began to loom before the men of Vichy with the hair-raising aspect of a resurrection from the dead. After considering all the eventualities, the Marshal himself made known among his intimates that he would stand or fall by German victory and that he had now decided that France must come more actively to the aid of Germany.

Seldom has treason gone farther than this. France must remain permanently enslaved, permanently the colony of a victorious Germany, in order to insure the safety and continued power of a regime which only emergency could have justified and which has grossly exceeded both the mandate and the wishes of the people from the moment of its inception. France must be compelled, if need be, by the men upon whom she depended for salvation, to tighten the chains which bind her, and to fight even the rescuer who now appears upon the horizon.

From its very beginnings, the Marshal reserved his sharpest condemnation for the De Gaullist movement and for the men who abandoned all hope of home and fortune to follow it. Having been ordered by this self-designated infallible mentor to bow their heads in resignation to the inevitability of defeat, they refused to recognize it, which was impious, and they have now been proved right, which is doubly intolerable. Each rise in the prospects of eventual Allied victory brings

an increased condemnation of the Fighting French movement, and punishment for suspected adherents no longer stops
with theoretical denationalization or property confiscations.
Long lists of hostages, charged only with being suspected
De Gaullists, are furnished to the Nazis, not by their own
spies alone but by Vichy police and by the Marshal's own
Garde Mobile. If the number of these alleged De Gaullists
released little by little from North African concentration
camps since the American landings—and apparently it runs
into thousands—can be taken as a guide, there must be in
France proper a wholesale incarceration both of De Gaullists
and of persons roughly labeled "Communist," a designation
covering a hundred shades of liberal and pro-French opinion.
At first the French people were disposed to accept some of
these arrests as necessary or as ordered under duress. But
truth, as always, is filtering through. And, as always, martyrdom is propagating faith. Both De Gaullists and Communists
are emerging from their persecution strengthened, allied, and
skilled in the devious arts of underground warfare.

When the cease-fighting order was given, it was applied
equally to metropolitan France and to her colonies. Nothing
obliged the colonies, since force of arms was not at that
moment forthcoming, to obey these orders, and large and
influential segments of the empire enlisted under the Cross
of Lorraine. To the others, principally those in North Africa,
Admiral Darlan had promptly dispatched men of his own
choosing, sailors whose careers he had made and who were
devoted to his interests. Then, as speedily as possible, "doubtful" civil administrators and their key subordinates were replaced by Darlanists. The transformation was rapid and
efficiently accomplished, and it was aided by the appointments, wherever they seemed necessary, of ambitious young

subalterns who had received orders to watch their chiefs for signs of independent action.

Germany chose judiciously among the mixture of ranks and types herded into her prison camps, in order to provide herself with useful agents in France. These were released and returned to their rejoicing families, with much trumpeting, for a sort of probationary period in which their value was thoroughly tested. Among these men, who to say the least had demonstrated no active dislike for Nazism, was General Dentz, who was an early return to the Marshal. The latter might reasonably have felt some suspicion for so high-ranking an officer amnestied with such honors by his captors. But apparently he did not, for General Dentz was immediately appointed military commandant of Syria, with full orders to defend it. Against whom? It was not likely that Germany would attack to obtain what in effect she already controlled. And it was still more unlikely that a French general whose captivity had been distinguished by the start of a friendship with Hitler would be disposed to oppose his new friends even if they did decide to acquire Syria openly by military force. And Dentz promptly proved the wisdom of his choice by hastening to offer the Germans whatever favors they required, including even the free use of Syrian airports, a concession far in excess of anything required by the armistice.

This move, in the minds of the Marshal and his advisers, was likely to have a beneficial effect upon the length of the war, since it would aid Nazi infiltration in the direction of the oil wells of Irak and Mosul and thus cut off a valuable British supply line. The need of this or some equivalent source of oil has been proved again since then by the ferocity of the German attack upon the Caucasus in each of the past three years. Had the Germans, with the willing aid of General Dentz, been able to seize these oil regions adjacent to Syria, their advantage might have meant the difference between eventual victory and immediate defeat.

But when the British took steps to resolve this menace, General Dentz fought bitterly and with more determination than he had displayed in May 1940, when the Germans were his opponents upon French soil. In every encounter thus far, the men of Vichy have shown themselves willing to fight far more vigorously and with a greater disregard for human life when their opponents have been the enemies of Germany than they did when, as the allies of England, they fought for the liberty of France. But none of the men around the Marshal had the remotest idea of fighting for French liberty. The mere idea that the masses of the French people might someday be free to express their views again fills their present rulers with foreboding.

By now even the most obstinate admirers of the Marshal have been forced to accept the truth. To him the armistice has been consistently, not a lamentable lesser of two evils, but a desirable end in itself, a means through which his own devious plans for the future of France and his own perpetuity in power might be achieved. The armistice procured nothing for France that a simple submission to armed force would not have obtained. France gained nothing through its dishonorable agreement with the conqueror. Only the Marshal and his clique of sycophants won. In the commission of this crime the answer to the question of who profits most is, and must be, Marshal Pétain.

It has been to Hitler's major interest to keep in power the men who so eagerly accepted capitulation. And it has been equally to their interest to make this capitulation a permanent factor in the disposition of France's future. This they have done with single-minded intensity. Far from encouraging the future liberators, the armies which one day might land upon French soil and restore the ravaged land to its people, the Marshal has attacked them verbally and with weapons upon every conceivable opportunity. While the Japanese hordes were welcomed as brothers in Indo-China, the British and the Free French have been attacked and fought off with all the violence at the command of those holding Syria, Dakar and Madagascar for the eventual use of the conquerors. No aid or encouragement has been given to the Frenchmen who slip away by night to join their brethren fighting for France. They are hunted as criminals and shot down as the basest of spies upon capture. But young Frenchmen have been exhorted to volunteer to wear the hated swastika and to die for Germany upon the Russian battlefields.

When Japanese intentions in regard to Indo-China became obvious, two Vichy colonels arrived in Washington to beg for arms. After the experience of Dakar and Syria, the State Department had grown increasingly wary of Vichy's need for munitions. Twice now the Pétain state had expended its stores against the principal ally of the United States, and England was keeping a sharp eye on requests for further favors. So a formal promise was demanded of the envoys, guaranteeing that the desired weapons would never be used against Great Britain. This was promptly and haughtily refused. The equipment would be used according to Vichy's best judgment. So the United States sought to find a formula that would not too abruptly rebuff the Marshal (this was still in the days when the wishful thinkers were convinced he was a noble old dupe who might be brought to be an ally) but that also would not gravely annoy the British. They remembered the hundred pursuit planes, stranded on Martinique since France capitulated, decaying unused while the fighting Allies sighed for planes and still more planes. So Washington suggested that these ships, theoretically no longer of use to the French, be returned in exchange for a hundred new ones which would be sent for the defense of Indo-China. This too was refused. The Curtiss planes stayed where they were, a potential threat to the Panama Canal, one of the useful elements in the blackmail plot, of which the United States had so far proved so patient a victim. So then the United States suggested that these planes be flown to Indo-China. This too was refused. The negotiations collapsed, the planes remained where they were, and when the Japanese negotiator appeared he was greeted with open arms. Not even a token resistance was offered, and the Japanese were handed the keys of the Pacific as honored partners in the New Order.

This incident was shrewdly motivated. It suggested to the United States the growing menace of Japan, implied that by diverting supplies from the European theater it would be empowering Vichy to meet the menace and tried subtly to plant the notion that Lend Lease aid to Great Britain and Russia was not protecting the best interest of this hemisphere. It aimed not alone at diverting a comparatively small cache of arms and planes to Vichy, but to suggest the much more important temptation that it would be better to keep supplies at home than to farm them out over the world. But the plan failed.

And Japan was granted by the Marshal all of the vast resources of French Indo-China without so much as the firing of a shot. Had France resisted Japanese occupation with the same determination she hurled against the British and their allies in Dakar, in Syria, in Madagascar and later in North

Africa, the Pacific war might have taken a different turn. Without Indo-China, Japan must have looked elsewhere for the springboard of its attack against Malaya, the Philippines and the Dutch Indies. Singapore might have had time to obtain reinforcements and, with the aid of retreating French forces, could have offered a more effective resistance. The two magnificent ships, the *Prince of Wales* and the *Repulse*, need not have been sacrificed in their desperate run toward the north. The Stars and Stripes might still be flying upon Bataan, and the precious Burma Road, main artery of China's war effort, need not have fallen into enemy hands. This is a formidable catalogue of effects to stem from the major cause of Vichy's close identification with the interests of the Axis.

For the ambition of Marshal Pétain and for the increasing cost of that ambition, thousands of young Americans have died or will have to die. Even if, by some turn of fate, an Allied landing in France should bring among the men of Vichy an eleventh-hour change of heart and an ostensible wish to side with the victor, the Marshal and his friends will never be able to wash out the effects of their previous actions or to offset the fact that they were willing to sell first France and then the liberties of all Europe in an effort to bolster their own slipping hopes and ambitions. The Marshal today prays for Nazi victory. He preaches a continuing crusade against Russia and fulminates incessantly of the evils of communism, as though any fate could be worse than the one he has willingly imposed upon Frenchmen. There is no further pretense of justice or a wise use of authority, and the sterile ideals upon which his personal new order was to be founded have fallen among the wider miseries which collaboration has visited upon France. He demands only an unquestioning and servile respect for his position and men who will accord him that are safe to pursue any scheme their cupidity or their plans for power may require. Balance his violent dislike of De Gaulle, Giraud, Catroux, Darlan and Tassigny against the approval still enjoyed, for instance, by the utterly incompetent General Corap, whom Reynaud accused with some justice of being personally responsible for the disaster at Sedan. General Corap is an obedient and docile servant of Vichy, and so his stupidity, his venality are matters of little moment in Vichy.

At the end of 1942 the last glimmering hope of a peace by Axis negotiation was extinct. For the American giant had awakened and had begun to fight. At Midway, on Guadalcanal and in Tunisia on the very doorstep of Europe, the sons of men who had fought at Yorktown, at Château-Thierry and in the Meuse-Argonne were proving worthy of their fathers. And now the aim of the accomplices, Hitler, Mussolini, Hirohito, Pétain and the handful of lesser quislings, was not a crushing peace by conquest or even the triumph of peace by arrangement, but a weary stalemate after the whole world was exhausted by war. From this might come at least safety and some security for the men who had made the war. For it began to look as though decisive victory, not too long delayed, was on the side of the Allies and if this were so the arrogant dreams of the erstwhile conquerors must be swallowed in a nightmare of blood and flame.

The landing in North Africa was perhaps even more decisive psychologically than materially. It demolished one of the most convincing of the Axis propaganda arguments used among wavering neutrals. This was the question: Granted that the United States might one day be able to measure its strength against that of the Axis, where would this great trial of strength be likely to take place? Hitler would certainly not be stupid enough to try to invade the Western Hemisphere and there was not one foot of the European continent where an army directed by other than suicidal maniacs would be likely to try to set foot. Europe was an armed camp, patrolled by Nazi soldiers. The possible danger spot of North Africa was safely entrusted to faithful Pétainists whose hopes and futures were bound up in Axis victory. Therefore, since there could be no battlefield, the United States was spending much money uselessly, and wise men would accept the facts of Axis victory.

But November 7 was a tremendous blow to this argument. It was, also, the last chance for the Marshal to prove that his patient friends and apologists were right, that his critics had been crushingly wrong. How he met this challenge the world now knows.

He might have won back at least a part of the world's and France's respect had he torn up the hateful armistice with his own hands and proclaimed that now the moral power of France, which no longer possessed any military power, was solidly behind the four great Allies. He might, less dramatically, merely have hinted that he had been mistaken about German invincibility. But in all his long life he had never admitted a mistake, never placed himself generously in the wrong and he was not to begin now. He might even, having no courage for open revolt, at least have remained silent, doing nothing to help perhaps, but at least nothing actively to hinder. Darlan seized his opportunity for rehabilitation swiftly enough and did not fear to admit earlier mistakes.

But the Marshal left no doubt of where his sympathies lay. Every angry word that could be spoken was uttered—against the Allies. Every incitement to fight and to resist was given—

against the Allies. A spark of the old energy of the days of
Verdun seemed to have returned, but it was directed, this
time, against the Allies. German troops appeared at Bizerte
before the Anglo-Americans, who were delayed, through
Pétain's orders, by the fighting directed by General Nogues
and Admiral Michelier. Thus Germany obtained the naval
base which had to be won back at the cost of months of
fighting and thousands of lives. Against Vichy's oft-repeated
claim that her soldiers were ordered to fight against any
invader, whoever he might be, stood the action of Admiral
Esteva, Pétain's naval governor of Bizerte, who handed over
to the German commander full power over the sea base and
the stronghold without the firing of a single shot. Admiral
Michelier, at the same time, fought for almost five days
against the friendly Americans.

Marshal Pétain is wholly and convincedly the willing ally
of the Fuehrer, and if France's collaboration must be enforced
by the iron rod, it is not his fault or the fault of his propa-
gandists. It is he who strives to keep in line for the benefit of
Germany the sullen workers who resist attempts to force them
into slavery for Germany. It is his police and agents who
endeavor to break up the small, brave parties of youths who
barricade themselves in mountain passes rather than be de-
ported to German factories. It is he who condones and even
aids the arrest and execution of hostages and underground
workers, who encourages the wholly un-French crime of anti-
Semitic persecution.

Admiral Darlan, with a praiseworthy personal loyalty, tried
to excuse the torrent of angry broadcasts by which the Marshal
in November 1942 strove to prevent French soldiers and
sailors from obeying Darlan, Giraud and Bethouard. The

Marshal, explained his erstwhile admiral, speaks under compulsion. Do not listen to his speeches, they are dictated by the enemy. The Marshal is a prisoner who speaks under the menace of constraint.

The excuse was demonstrably thin, but the intention was kind. It did not seem credible that so old a man could fear death. He had accepted in his first speech the possibility of sacrificing what remained of his life for France. Indeed, in this broadcast he had not scrupled to compare his possible fate with that of a far greater Giver of His life: "We offer our person in sacrifice to France," he had announced, using the regal form in a travesty of humility.

In answer to Admiral Darlan, the Marshal replied and in unmistakable terms rebuked the presumption that any force controlled his utterance:

"To dare to say that I speak or act under the menace or under the empire of duress is an insult to me!"

Thus the Marshal assumed full responsibility for his words and his deeds. And in doing so he merely echoed Hitler himself, who, on November 12, 1942, had written in the words of one confederate to another:

"It is well known to me, Herr Marshal, that you yourself have always been and still are a faithful partisan of the collaboration of France with National-Socialist Germany. . . ."

Thus Henri Philippe Pétain is condemned by himself and by his arch accomplice. He it is who has betrayed France with premeditation, with persistence and with no shadow of remorse. The oldest and most renowned of her living heroes, he has proved also the oldest and most notorious of those who deliberately plotted her ruin. And his sharpest punishment may well be, should his life endure so long, the sight of the long lines of French warriors, united behind leaders whose faith has never wavered, marching once again beneath the Arc de Triomphe and resurrecting, in the name of their fathers who sleep forever at Verdun, the name and the honor of the fair land of France.

INDEX